Light on the Path
For Awakening

LIGHT ON THE PATH FOR AWAKENING

A COMMENTARY ON MABEL COLLINS' SPIRITUAL CLASSIC

SWAMI NIRMALANANDA GIRI
(ABBOT GEORGE BURKE)

LIGHT of the SPIRIT
PRESS
CEDAR CREST, NEW MEXICO

Published by
Light of the Spirit Press
lightofthespiritpress.com

Light of the Spirit Monastery
P. O. Box 1370
Cedar Crest, New Mexico 87008
OCOY.org

ISBN paperback: 978-1-955046-28-2
ISBN epub: 978-1-955046-29-9

Library of Congress Control Number: 2024939213

Bisac categories:

1. REL068000   RELIGION / Theosophy

2. OCC016000 BODY, MIND & SPIRIT / Occultism

3. SEL032000   SELF-HELP / Spiritual

4. OCC031000 BODY, MIND & SPIRIT / Ancient Mysteries & Controversial Knowledge

1st edition

01192025

CONTENTS

Introduction vii

Part 1 1

Part 2 108

Appendix: Soham Yoga 179

Glossary 185

About the Author 190

INTRODUCTION

In the last quarter of the nineteenth century, an Englishwoman named Mabel Collins printed a small book on the beginnings of the spiritual quest entitled *Light On The Path*. She did not consider herself the author but only the transmitter. Therefore she insisted that the title page say: "Written down by M. C."

Since a well-known esoteric organization that claimed to be disciples of hidden masters, both physical and disembodied, insisted that her book had really been psychically dictated to her by one of their masters, she wrote the following to establish the truth of the matter: "I ought further to state that *Light on the Path* was not to my knowledge inspired by anyone; but that I saw it written on the walls of a place I visit spiritually–there I read it and I wrote it down."

Light on the Path explains the nature of discipleship and the qualities of a worthy disciple. The master of such a disciple is the disciple's own divine Self which draws its existence from the Supreme Self: God. Though we may have many teachers, some of them even divinized sons of God, nevertheless ultimately on the Path only God and the Soul alone are anyone's masters. It is good to keep this in mind when reading *Light on the Path*. However, we will also consider interaction and obligation in relation to lesser teachers than God and the spirit-Self.

Whenever in this commentary I cite Jesus, either his words or his example, I do so with the understanding that Jesus is a great siddha as were Krishna, Buddha and others of the great masters that have appeared in this world.

The following commentary carefully analyzes her transcription, for those who would make the Great Journey must know both the path and how to travel upon it.

PART ONE

I. These rules are written for all disciples: Attend you to them.

Before the eyes can see, they must be incapable of tears. Before the ear can hear, it must have lost its sensitiveness. Before the voice can speak in the presence of the Masters it must have lost the power to wound. Before the soul can stand in the presence of the Masters its feet must be washed in the blood of the heart.

These rules are written for all disciples.

What is a disciple? The Greek word *mathetes* which in the Bible is translated "disciple" means "one who is learning." Many study and many experience, but few learn. A disciple is one who does learn. The Sanskrit word *shishya* translated "disciple" in Indian scriptures is more like the English term. It literally means "one who is under discipline."

A genuine disciple is not living by his whim, but according to the guidelines set forth by the wise of all ages. They are rules, a word based on the Latin *regula*, from which we get the word "regulate," which means to control, to rule something. In this case we are to rule our own lower nature, mind and intellect. So the path of the disciple is the path of discipline. Such a one both allows himself to be disciplined and actually disciplines himself. It is also the path of obedience in the sense of free acquiescence to the counsels of the wise, but it is not the fearful slavishness usually demanded by the forces of the world: religious, economic or political.

The path of spiritual discipleship is rigorous and requires an equally rigorous preparation. Let us begin a prudent accounting of all the aspects of discipleship.

First, of course is discipline itself. Disciples are those who actively follow a regimen of self-purification to clarify their minds and thus make themselves capable of receiving higher knowledge. They must prepare themselves so that when they are given wisdom they will both recognize it and be able to apply it.

Saying that "these rules are written for all disciples" means that there are absolutely no exceptions to them. Some people are always looking for shortcuts or the easy way, but such things do not exist in this realm of highest truth. What is written is written for all.

Attend you to them.

The will is the most important factor in the makeup of any evolving entity. It is the supreme power wielded by the evolving individual. Free will is freely spoken of, but a truly free will is rare indeed, and not to be had for the mere wishing or talking.

The basic requisite of the disciple is the freeing and empowering of his will. This is done through discipline and obedience that are not imposed upon the disciple but freely and willingly taken up, that are acts of will rather than surrendering of will. To be truly freeing, discipline and obedience can spring solely from one motivation: the attainment of divine consciousness. Therefore they cannot be engaged in from either fear of pain and punishment or hope of reward. Nor should they be taken up because of having become intellectually convinced or emotionally cajoled by any external or internal forces, including ego, emotions, intellect or desires. The disciple must come to know and understand the rules. From that moment on the following of those rules must be a spontaneous response arising from his own Self–from nowhere else and from nothing else whatsoever.

The real spiritual masters leave their pupils free to follow wisdom or not. Neither with words nor with silence do they seek to influence them. For true freedom, the freedom of the spirit, this is a requisite. That is why in the closing section of the Bhagavad Gita, Krishna says to Arjuna: "Thus has the knowledge that is more secret than all that is secret been expounded to you by me. Having reflected on this fully, act in the way you wish" (Bhagavad Gita 18:63).

Before the eyes can see, they must be incapable of tears.

Tears are expressions of intense and uncontrolled emotional reaction to something. They occur when people are happy, sad, frustrated, afraid, angry or overwhelmed by some experience. They can result from experiencing great beauty or great repulsion. So what is really being talked about here is being overcome by egoic reactions, which are symbolized by tears.

The Master is not ordering us to become emotionless, but to always be masters of our emotions; to never let ourselves be carried away by them. Otherwise our minds will be confused and our intelligence clouded. As Krishna warns in the Gita: "From destruction of intelligence one is lost" (Bhagavad Gita 2:63).

We are not to become emotionless zombies. There are those who read about how the world is unreal and we must be detached. Trying to realize this ideal they become emotionally unresponsive and dead. I have known people who would not show affection to their own spouses or children because they feared "negative attachment." This rule is not advocating such unnatural fanaticism. It is not advocating the eradication of love, compassion, mercy, generosity and suchlike, but the eradication of selfishness and its emotional tempests that arise either from pleasure or displeasure. We cannot possibly maintain the life of a disciple until we have become actually incapable of this egoic type of response.

There is also a higher meaning to being "incapable of tears." We must become incapable of being hurt or grieved by anything upon this earth, incapable of reacting to external objects (which include a lot that we consider internal) with sorrow, disappointment, disgust, frustration, anger, fear or grief. In other words, the negativity of this world must not move us to respond, especially in kind. We must never feel helpless and frustrated by the nightmares shown us in the dream-theater we mistakenly call "the real world." We must become unmoved by the false appearances of material existence: not from emotional deadness but from understanding their fundamental unreality.

We must become incapable of being swept away by seemingly positive reactions to earthly phenomena as well, for human beings often shed tears of joy as well as sorrow. In short, we must become unmoved by the ever-shifting scenes of this earthly dream-existence, and become anchored in the peace and joy of the Spirit.

There is another aspect to this. Tears distort the vision and blind the eyes. Tears come between the eye, the organ of perception, and whatever should be perceived. So we are being warned that unless we have entered this "tearless" state there is a chance that as we pursue the divine vision our inner eye may have its vision blotted out or distorted by the intervention of these "tears" between us and that which is true.

There is an ancient story of a prince who upon becoming king was visited by a sage who gave him a ring upon which were engraved the words: "Even This Must Pass Away." Throughout his life, when he would be about to be overcome by elation, desire, anger or sadness, his eyes would light upon those words and he would immediately regain the right perspective and remain calm. Then at the moment of his death he was fearless as he gazed upon the assurance that: "Even This Must Pass Away."

Before the ear can hear, it must have lost its sensitiveness.

We are not to become deaf. Our inner ear must be able to hear, but it should hear only one thing: the voice of the spirit. But to become sensitive to the voice of higher consciousness we must become insensitive to extraneous things, to stop being responsive to material life and the resultant material consciousness. We must perfectly–that is, intelligently–disregard all potential distractions.

This is especially true in the matter of social consciousness or peer pressure. There are people who would go to lingering death rather than transgress social rules or be thought ill of by those around them. People are far more afraid of looking bad than they are of actually being bad. Especially in modern times other people's eyes are the mirrors that determine how we come to see ourselves. For this reason Sri Ramakrishna often told His disciples that those who were subject to fear and shame could never know God.

Those who are "in step with the times" are naturally out of step with eternity. Those who are influenced by every worldly wind and tide are beyond the sphere of divine communication. Those who are always fully up on all the latest fashion, verbal jargon, events, fads, trends and interests are the high priests and priestesses of world-worship.

Contemporary religion is poisoned with this sensitivity and reflexive responsiveness to any earthly absurdity. Some years back we used to get a monthly newsletter from a (supposedly) spiritual group. One day a very tiny item appeared in our local newspaper about women in the East Coast deciding that they wanted to be called "Ms." Within the week the newsletter came filled with Ms. here and Ms. there. It was obvious they had completely retyped the copy to accommodate such nonsense without even waiting to see if it would catch on. (It did.) The secular masters (mistresses in this case) had whistled, and like well-trained dogs they had come to heel. Being aliens to the world of spirit, this material earth is the only world such persons know or care about, so they bend into conformity at every wind that blows over it. The Beloved Disciple had it right when he wrote: "They are of the world: therefore speak they of the world, and the world heareth them" (I John 4:5).

Our ears must be attuned only to the voice of wisdom. Then alone are we really free. We can have no standards other than those of spiritual life if we would succeed in the life of the spirit. This includes being unresponsive to our own lower nature and responsive only to our higher, divine Self. It also includes our refusal to be controlled by supposed duties or obligations originating in the world and the ego, and instead looking upon the things of the spirit alone as mandatory.

Many people use their supposed obligations and worldly responsibilities to neglect or altogether abandon spiritual life. Yet in an instant they throw over those earthly ties to fulfill personal and material desires or ambitions. This is especially true in family life. These individuals pretend to be morally enslaved to children, spouse, or parents—especially if those relatives do not like their spiritual activities. They make quite a production of how they cannot be so heartless as to upset them or spoil their relationship by doing something objectionable, or how afraid they are of their displeasure and censure. But if you can spend some time with them you will find them snapping orders at these very people and constantly hurting them with complete callousness. Still, when spiritual life comes up they begin to figuratively limp around and whine as though they were under the total domination of those they use as an excuse. And woe to those who indicate that such "obligations" are not legitimate reasons to slack off, for they will be denounced as heartless monsters who want them to hurt their loved ones or break up their familial harmony.

It is also true that there are those who refuse to fulfill their legitimate obligations under the cloak of spirituality. This is perhaps even more despicable.

There are also those that play a double game of deception and irresponsibility. They neglect their duties to their families and livelihood under the pretense that they are devoting their time to spiritual life. Then they neglect their spiritual duties under the pretense that they are having to fulfill their obligations to their families: a neat trick that often succeeds in bamboozling both sides, each thinking that the other is the cause of their neglect, while both are being shirked.

The disciple must avoid all these excuses and pitfalls.

Before the voice can speak in the presence of the Masters it must have lost the power to wound.

The very capacity for negative speaking must be eliminated. The voice, which is much more than just words, being also thought and will, must lose the power to injure either ourselves or others through misapplication, falsehood, evil-speaking, slander, insult, cruelty, harshness or the desire to injure verbally. It also includes trying to manipulate other people.

Before the soul can stand in the presence of the Masters its feet must be washed in the blood of the heart.

"Stand" means to be established in a definite position, to be bold and firm. Therefore the blood of the heart has to be shed. The heart must be opened and its blood poured out just as Saint Mary Magdalene poured the sweet perfume on the head of Jesus (Matthew 26:6-7).

You can bleed from other places and survive, but if you pierce open the heart and it bleeds, you are on the way to death. So we are being exhorted to purify ourselves through the martyrdom of the ego. Just as the Mayans cut out the hearts of victims and offered them in sacrifice, so we must cut out the ego to right away strike at the very thing that has been keeping us running away from God throughout so many lives. We must cut out our own heart, so to speak. We must shed our own blood. But when we do so we shall not die but live, for we shall discover that the ego is not our heart after all, but that our true heart is our immortal spirit. We will find our life is not in the blood of egotism, but in God. So our seeming inner suicide will really be our resurrection. "For whoever desires to save his life will lose it, but whoever loses his life for My sake will find it" (Matthew 16:25).

False identity has so gripped us that only by such drastic means will we be freed. "When the 'I' shall die, then shall I know who am I," said Paramhansa Yogananda. Sad to say, many people start out in spiritual life and then quit when it becomes a little bit inconvenient, troublesome, embarrassing, uncomfortable or difficult. But disciples must be otherwise.

To this end we must give our heart's blood, to unreservedly pour out the very essence of our life which, as already said, will then be seen to not have been our life at all, for we shall then come to know God as our life. What a joyous prospect!

1. Kill out ambition.
2. Kill out desire of life.
3. Kill out desire of comfort.
4. Work as those work who are ambitious.

1. Kill out ambition.

It is ego-based ambition that is being spoken of here. We must not merely suppress such ambition, we must annihilate it. Obviously the worthy disciple has worthy goals which he attempts to realize. What is prohibited is ambition in the sense of wanting to gain some position or object which will please the short-sighted ego. To believe that any gain or position in the external material world is of lasting value is in itself a terrible delusion and is sure to produce conflict in spiritual life, for the attitudes requisite for (egoic) success in the material and in the spiritual planes are often opposite in character.

One side of this proscription is actually practical, even in an earthly sense, for it also means that a person should not overreach himself but live within his means materially. According to this view bigger is not better, and continual unrestrained growth is not progress. This is the terrible economic tiger we are riding today. There is a constant clamoring for increase of "the gross national product," etc. Although the Law of Diminishing Returns is well known as a theory, no one is applying it on a large scale to economic and social growth. Therefore our economy is like the bullfrog that kept puffing itself up more and more until it exploded. This constant pressure for advancement, for bigger and better, is a terrible roller coaster that is sure to dump us eventually, and in between we suffer terrible anxieties.

Ambition as the desire for adulation from others is also delusive. Ambition for material gain stems from the delusion that the more we have the more we are: it is a matter of false self-identity. Ambition for notoriety springs from the mistaken idea that we are what other people think of us. In other words, anything that gives an egoic adulation, or an egoic satisfaction, produces a false identity. The one identity we should have is that we are a disciple, one who is treading the path toward the Real.

Egoic ambition is an indication that the individual does not know his real nature, but is struggling to establish or conform to a false self-concept. The effect of this is that he works to become something imaginary in his own eyes, rather than to manifest the reality of his divine nature. He wants to become something in the world, to have a flattering label applied to him. Such persons have very little interior personal development but are a shallow bundle of "interpersonal skills." These people become the leaders of even shallower people.

In the university I did a study on personality aspects and had access to the records of psychological tests given to the students. This included the records of the class officers and various "big" men and women on campus. The tests showed consistently that the leaders and the "socially skilled" were far less developed interiorly (self-image, emotional stability, etc.) than was normal. On the other hand, those whose scores indicated very high self-development consistently scored below normal in socially-oriented areas. It was most revealing. The leaders and "great guys" all had extremely low self-esteem, therefore they needed others to tell them something about themselves that they did not even believe. Those who were emotionally stable simply did not need to manipulate others into assuring them of what they already knew about themselves. Ergo, they were "socially unskilled." From this it became evident that social skills meant methods of manipulation, not genuine friendliness or the ability to really care about others. In contrast, the leaders on campus used others as mere echo chambers, mirrors in which they admired their own (self-disliked) faces. "How skillful human beings are in their ignorance," Yogananda also said.

My study also revealed that the supposed leaders were really followers. That is, they were simply jackanapes, monkeys on a string that gained popularity by merely feeding to their admirers what they wanted to see and hear. At the other end of the spectrum were those who needed no such "other direction," but like the wise of all ages could in truth Know, Will, Dare and Be Silent. Being highly developed inwardly, they scored low on the social side because they were not interested in running other people. They were not crude in their behavior or without friends, but they were centered in living their own life, and being alive inside.

Not only is earthly ambition to be eliminated, so also must spiritual ambition.

On a more metaphysical level, spiritual ambition is often an indication of pride. Often when people read books on spiritual life, especially lives of great saints and masters, they are attracted to the glamorous phenomena and imagine themselves being so powerful or so admired. It is not real spiritual life that is attracting them at all. As a result, they may try a little spiritual practice, but they give it up early on when it does not produce the thrills, chills and overnight glory they expected.

During my first trip to India I met a great yogi, Sitaramdas Omkarnath. Just to be in his presence was purifying and blessed. A man who was with me formed the same opinion about his greatness, but on a much different basis. He rhapsodized over how many rich and important people had been there showing respect to the saint! "Just think," he kept saying to me, "a Brigadier General in the Indian Army showed him such respect. He must be really great!"

When we read of the great ones our egos tend to blind us to the great sacrifices and discipline required of them to reach their high level, and we only think of the miracle-working or the notoriety gained. Forgetting the price, we aspire to be saints as well. But the truth is, we are not interested in being saints, we are only interested in having their notoriety and glory. Saint Seraphim of Sarov is very popular because he shone with light, floated in the air and cured sickness. But very few want to undergo the tremendous struggles and hardships that were the refining fires in which his spiritual gold was made pure. They forget his persecutions by fellow monks, his physical illnesses and the occasions when he nearly died from injuries, both natural and from evil men. Also they forget his decades of strict solitude, never leaving his room or speaking to others. Yet those things are the realities of his sanctity, for they reveal his desire and love for God. Spiritual ambition, being based on egotism, breeds impatience in spiritual practice. That is why Yogananda often said: "A saint is a sinner who never gave up."

2. Kill out desire of life.

It is hard to speak more plainly or more drastically than this. First, this means to kill out all desire for our mistaken ideas of what constitutes life. How often we hear people speak about "really living," when they are actually only diverting themselves from life through frenetic activities.

Whatever our erroneous definitions of life may be, they have one thing in common, from the coarsest to the most sophisticated, subtle and even philosophical: they consist of becoming absorbed in objective consciousness. And that absorption constitutes death in the form of the loss of subjective consciousness: real Self-consciousness.

Life being spiritual in essence, it must be a state of full and unimpaired internal awareness. This does not mean that being alive means to be in some kind of perpetual trance, unaware of the external world. Rather, it means to move and function easily and competently amidst all outer conditions and objects while at the same time maintaining perfect interior awareness. The truly alive person is unshakably established in the center of his being, his pure consciousness or spirit, while at the same time working out his evolution through interaction with the environment produced by his individual karmas. It is the difference between swimming in the ocean and drowning in it.

So to kill out the desire of life means to free ourselves from all illusions regarding its constitution. It is not an exhortation to become a zombie or automaton, just the opposite. By freeing ourselves from mistaken definitions of life we can then begin to discover the truth of its nature. We are not told kill out desire *for* life, but desire *of* life—the many delusive desires that our misperceptions of life produce in us. For what is "life" as we presently experience it? It is this moving picture of ever-changing conditions that surrounds us. Although it is meant to be an instrument of teaching, a kind of grand-scale training film, it still is basically an illusion. To reach out into the illusion in the vain hope of taking something to ourselves that will either satisfy or really change us is just that: a vain hope.

When I was a little child I had a really silly delusion. I believed that if I saw something in a dream that I wanted (and I always knew when I was dreaming), I need only hold on to it tightly as I sensed myself awakening and I could bring it out of the dream and into my waking life. To a child of the 'forties, Woolworth's Dime Store was a paradise. Often I would dream I was in Woolworth's and able to take anything I wanted. I would wander around, picking out various items, carrying them with me. Then as I felt myself awakening, I would hold on to them, pressing them tightly to my chest. When awake, I would look to see if I had succeeded, but would always be disappointed. "You can't take it with you" is true in all dreams. And since to be "in the spirit" is to be awake, it therefore follows that we cannot bring anything of the delusive dream-world into it.

The various external objects we encounter in life are like bait, and the desire for them is the hook that catches us, the unwary fish that try to swallow them and somehow assimilate them into our lives. We are pulled out of ourselves and suffocated like the hapless fish. The truth about earthly life is that it steals us, we do not steal it. It possesses us rather than our possessing it. Those who believe they have gained so much in life have actually become enslaved, for they are owned by those things.

This world is like the tar baby of Uncle Remus. When we grab for it, we stick to it. Then it seizes us and whirls us around to wherever it wants us to go. But we can be so deluded that we think we are doing it all ourselves. The world seizes us, shapes us into its own image and pushes us around just like puppets, and all the while we brag about our free will.

Perhaps the most important aspect of the directive to kill out desire of life is the cutting off of the delusion that external objects can change us, making us something other than what we are in our essential and eternal nature. Although we can make objects come into our temporary life sphere, since all relative existence in based on duality the very coming implies an eventual going. Whatever is gained must eventually be lost: getting implies losing. Therefore nothing can ever become "ours" in any real sense at all. This is not only true of the physical, but of the subtle worlds and levels of our being as well, The "desires of life" proceed from a false identity and a false self-concept. To realize who and what we really are we must clear aside the veils of these desire-illusions.

Finally, we need to notice that the rule implies we have the ability to kill out desire of life, that it is not something beyond our strength or capacity. Also, the command is not to deny, turn from, or reject desire of life, but to *destroy* it. That is because if we do not destroy it, it will arise to hinder us in the future.

Since both desire and ambition usually manifest through action, let us consider action itself. The basic problem with action is our inability to act without the idea: "I am doing this." As a consequence there is no action, however small, that cannot become an egoic trap for us. Thus, every moment of our life we run the risk of egoic illusion, of taking any action however insignificant and making it seem significant, using it as an avenue for ego. Moreover, other people are usually involved in our actions, even if only in the capacity of observers who are going to pass judgement on the action. And this automatically calls forth egoic reactions on our part.

We are especially sensitive to the opinions of others regarding our deeds. Whether it is criticism or praise from others, the ego becomes hooked by it and begins to react. So then, how do we act in discharging our duties, etc.? Actually, the solution is quite simple: it is a matter of placement of consciousness. If we are centered in our lower selves or in the action we shall surely fall into the delusions of egotism. But if our consciousness is centered in God, the sole Doer, then we shall be safe. What is more, we will do our work much better than otherwise! This has been observed through the ages. Those who keep their minds on God as they go about their daily routine are seen to do everything much better than those who get lost in self-involvement or "work consciousness."

3. Kill out desire of comfort.

This needs to be done on all levels: physical, psychological and spiritual. By "comfort" is meant ease. On the physical level it includes luxury. But the main idea is the desire for comfort in the sense of everything being easy and without effort. We must kill out such a desire because the spiritual path is not easy. The moment struggle ceases, at that moment life and evolution cease.

> Does the road wind up-hill all the way?
>> Yes, to the very end.
> Will the day's journey take the whole long day?
>> From morn to night, my friend.

The rod does in truth wind uphill all the way—yes, to the very end.

Since we get whatever we want, if we desire spiritual ease we will get it. But it will be spiritual stagnation, as well. Spiritual life is not for a person who wants to find peace in the sense of a lack of struggle. Spiritual life is really a very ruthless and relentless war. Only when there is total victory is there peace and cessation from "troubles." Only after long battles do we gain the ultimate peace of liberation.

In a war the good soldier lays his whole life "on the line." There is no other way to fight worthily. He who would save his life by holding back or evading conflict and sacrifice shall lose it. But he who gives up his life in total dedication to the endeavor shall find his life and save it. No price is too high. Those who have their top price beyond which they will not go will eventually reach it and fall by the way.

Contentment is not for the disciple. Rather, he must be seized with divine discontent, desiring to strive ever onward and upward, ceasing not until the Goal is fully won. Those who demand assurance that they will be successful, or who insist that someone hold their hand and comfort them, telling them that all will be well and that it will be worth it, can only fail in spiritual life. For their problem is that they do not really want spiritual life at all. The same is true of those who constantly demand explanations and justifications of the requirements and disciplines of spiritual life. Those who must be wheedled and coaxed are thoroughly unworthy. And those who demand special concessions and special treatment should not even be considered.

We must always be stirred up to action and moving steadily along the spiritual path. Otherwise we will stagnate and die. We are like the fish that must keep moving otherwise they will suffocate. So there can be no wish for ease and comfort. Comfortable religion is the worst possible thing we can get caught up in. Real religion discomfits us and gets us moving on to God. Also, since spiritual life involves struggle and (seeming) sacrifice, those who demand comfort will condition themselves to reject spiritual life.

As with the other things that must be cut off, the desire for comfort stems from the belief that peace and satisfaction are external conditions. By weaning ourselves from these delusions we come to understand that all we are looking for outside ourselves is to be found within. And when we quit looking for these things from an outside source we will be enabled to find what we want–and more–within.

We are constantly externalizing our consciousness in order to perceive and relate to the outside world. We must now reverse the process in order to develop internal perceptions. And then do you know what we will discover? We will find that instead of losing awareness of the outer world we will come to see it with a clarity heretofore undreamed of. In fact, we will come to perceive it perfectly. And this is because the outer proceeds from the inner, it is actually a reflection of the inner reality. That is the secret! But only those who are willing to turn within discover that. Only those who are willing to give it all up, to sacrifice it, will really gain it. All others will spend their lives grasping for it, only to eventually be swept away on the tide of death and lose everything (which they never really had anyway, such is the cruel irony).

In the very beginning of my awakening and search I discovered that right away I was more alive, content and optimistic than I had ever been. One day I went with some friends into a small restaurant by the university campus. We sat down in a booth and off to the side I saw a chubby black-bespectacled student with a sour angry face. After a few minutes he came rushing over and pushed his way into the booth until he was facing me. "Every time I see you, you are always having fun!" he spat accusatorially. "And I don't like it! I never have fun and why should you?" If I had told him why, he would not have believed it–about either his misery or my happiness. So I just smiled and one of my friends suggested that he vacate the spot. Which he did. But when we came out of the restaurant he was standing there and kept watching us like a thundercloud as we got in a car and drove off.

In her book *The Scent of Water* Elizabeth Goudge tells of a thief who reformed and became a hermit. As part of his penance he built a beautiful chapel, and at the back carved a self-portrait in which he was crowned with thorns. But those who looked closely saw that there was a gap between the thorns and the head of the carving; and when they put their fingers behind the carved thorns they could feel that the monk was really crowned with roses! And so it is. When the lower self tries to lead the life of the spirit it is an awful struggle that is doomed to fail. But when we let our spirit (and therefore, God) begin to unfold the divine life it is comparatively easy and inevitable. Just as you cannot eat with your elbow, you cannot lead the life of the spirit with anything but the spirit; and the spirit is able to utilize all the lesser elements of our being as tools for success. We need never doubt or fear: it is our destiny to manifest divinity.

4. Work as those work who are ambitious. Respect life as those who desire it. Be happy as those are who live for happiness.

Work as those work who are ambitious.

This is a most important principle, since many people think that in spiritual life we must turn into jellyfish. But we must work, for it is our karma to engage in various actions. And by so doing we free ourselves from the bonds of karma. If we avoid those actions, however, then the karma must be fulfilled in a future time, even a future life. There is no escape! However, since it is our karma that certain actions must be fulfilled, we should work at them very well, but without ambition. Notice that the directive is to work as those who have ambition. In other words, we have no ambition, but we must work as skillfully and energetically as if we did—not carelessly or irresponsibly.

This applies to spiritual life, as well. We must not have spiritual ambition (this also is a delusion), but we must work at it as steadily and doggedly as if we did. We continually see how dedicated and willing to struggle and sacrifice are those who have worldly ambition. We must observe and learn from them, for since the material world reflects the spiritual world, the same rules apply in both. We must have the same drive, but for spiritual life.

We must expend all our energies in the pursuit of spiritual perfection. When Sri Ramakrishna asked one of his teachers if he was mad, she answered: "My son, some people are mad for the world, and you are mad for God." So great must our intensity be that we may truly be said to be cracked on divine life. There is no place for cowardly or lazy "moderation" in this ideal.

By fulfilling even our non-spiritual tasks as well as we can, we are fitting ourselves for success in spiritual life. As Sri Ramakrishna said: "If you can weigh salt, you can weigh sugar." That is, if you are proficient in one kind of life you will be skilled in the other. And since we usually cannot see the inner realms of the spirit, we can use our outer life as a barometer of the spirit. For the principle "as above so below" applies here as well. If we are careless or incompetent in our physical work, we are deficient in our inner work. When a person cannot even walk a straight line, you know that he cannot think in a straight line, either. Only the lazy and the fake would have us think otherwise. If we cannot scrape a carrot, trim off the ends, cut it up, and boil it, how then are we possibly going to do such an amazing thing as expand our consciousness to an infinite capacity? If we cannot water a house plant, what will we do in spiritual life? If the mind cannot do such a simple thing, then higher life is impossible.

One sign of correct meditation is the developing of the ability to function in material life. As we become spiritually effective and efficient, so do we in the outer life as well. At one period in her life Madame Blavatsky successfully started a series of businesses, including an ink factory! She would begin a business, develop it into a success, and then sell it and begin another. Her relatives thought she was a fool, but she was doing it all as an exercise in spiritual life. By so doing she demonstrated her spiritual proficiency and set the example for those who would aspire to her level of attainment. No one could accuse her of not being able to make her way in the world. Just before coming to America she completed a tremendously successful tour through Russia and Europe as a concert pianist under the stage name of "Madame Laura"!

Respect life as those who desire it.

Life is not to be despised, including the life of earthly incarnation. Quite the opposite, it is to be respected and valued because it is a teacher. It must be preserved and cared for. This applies to the life of others, as well. This world is like a motion picture: just the play of light and shadow upon the screen of universal consciousness. But we do not disdain it, for it is an educational film. We must pay close attention to it and take its message very seriously. We must apply ourselves to it as though it were real, while retaining the awareness of its evanescent dream nature. Those who believe it is real are the ones who fail. The only ones who can really succeed are those who know that it is unreal and go ahead and apply themselves to it with the divine perspective. Thus the divine energies and divine intelligence within begin to manifest in the life of the individual. This is the secret of success in life.

So then, life in all its aspects is not to be desired, but it is to be respected. It is to be taken seriously without believing in it for a moment, just as we would seriously help a child work through an imaginary problem. It would be a mistake to refuse to help the child even though the problem is nonexistent, and equally a mistake to become like the child in thinking that there is a real problem. Our approach must be seemingly contradictory.

In the Bhagavad Gita Krishna points out to Arjuna that he works ceaselessly yet is never attached to anything. "I have no duty whatsoever in the three worlds, nor anything that must be attained, nevertheless I engage in action" (Bhagavad Gita 3:22). So it must be with us who are reflections of God. God creates and maintains the world, yet at no time is drawn into it or caught in it. Never is he controlled or conditioned or affected by it, since he is its Source and knows that eventually it is to be dissolved. Creation responds to God, but God does not respond to creation though absolutely intent on it. Since we are learning to be consciously united with God and share his life and consciousness (the two are really one), this is part of the learning process, of practicing how to participate in the Being of God.

Much as we should desire to return to the Source we should not desire to end incarnate existence, either here or in the higher worlds, until we have fully developed the capacities that the incarnate condition is intended to produce. It is senseless to abandon the class until the lesson is learned. Therefore life must be engaged in without ever being caught up in it.

Be happy as those are who live for happiness.

Living for happiness is a spontaneous, completely natural way of living in the happiness (bliss: ananda) that is really the essential nature of existence itself. Those who seek happiness artificially are never really happy, because they think that happiness comes from an external result or from a physical condition or situation, whereas there is no real contentment to be derived from an external object. This is because all external objects are material, and we are exclusively spiritual in nature. Therefore contentment can only be found in the spirit. Neither material nor psychological objects can satisfy us, for we are neither body nor mind. And it is an especially deadly delusion to equate pleasure with happiness.

To reach outward for happiness is to eventually be disappointed and therefore suffer. Instead, we must be happy inwardly, resting in the divine perfection of our inner Self, the immortal spirit. Happiness is within because the spirit is within. We already are perfectly at ease, in balance, in harmony, at rest, and contented—but only in the spirit. In one sense we are not just happy, we are happiness itself; we are not just conscious, we are consciousness itself; we are not just alive, we are life itself. Happiness is dwelling in the consciousness that is the Self. Otherwise we will be like the musk deer that smells the fragrance emanating from its own body and rushes around wildly, exhausting itself in the search for the source of the perfume. How many of us have searched for an item of clothing we were already wearing or looked for an object that was right in our hand? So it is with happiness, indeed with life itself in its fulness.

Seek in the heart the source of evil and expunge it. It lives fruitfully in the heart of the devoted disciple as well as in the heart of the man of desire. Only the strong can kill it out. The weak must wait for its growth, its fruition, its death. And it is a plant that lives and increases throughout the ages. It flowers when the man has accumulated unto himself innumerable existences. He who will enter upon the path of power must tear this thing out of his heart. And then the heart will bleed, and the whole life of the man seem to be utterly dissolved. This ordeal must be endured: it may come at the first step of the perilous ladder which leads to the path of life: it may not come until the last. But, O disciple, remember that is has to be

endured, and fasten the energies of your soul upon the task. Live neither in the present nor the future, but in the eternal. This giant weed cannot flower there: this blot upon existence is wiped out by the very atmosphere of eternal thought.

Seek in the heart the source of evil and expunge it.

That is only intelligent policy, isn't it? False spiritual life is that which neither has nor is intended to have any lasting positive effect on the individual. The ego produces it in infinite variety whatever the religious tradition. But all the varieties have a common denominator: they do not actually remove the source of evil from the individual consciousness. The symptoms of evil may be momentarily hidden or suppressed, but the evil itself is not removed by false "seeking."

Just as incompetent medicine pays attention to the symptoms only and not to the disease that is the source of the symptoms, so does ignorant religion in the spiritual realm. And just as modern medicine often treats only the symptoms with the mistaken premise that if the symptoms disappear the disease has been removed, so also does its spiritual counterpart, ignorant religion. Ignorant religion also engages in the production of artificial "positive" behavior with the idea that you are what you act like you are, that if you can manage to glitter you have thereby become gold!

One of the reasons such delusive religion sells so well throughout the world is that it keeps the consciousness confined to the superficial levels of external consciousness where no real change is possible. To maintain its dominion over us, the ego is determined that we shall not have interior awareness. For the thing that the ego fears the most is interior awakening. Therefore it leads the seeker into illusory byways. Some evil people go into an absolute tailspin the moment they hear that someone wants to practice meditation. They begin to throw all kinds of verbal bombs at the poor aspirant, insisting that meditation is selfish, impractical, mentally harmful and such like. Their overreaction tells us that they are afraid of meditation because the inner consciousness it produces strikes at the very root of the evil to which they are polarized.

It is essential to realize that the root of evil is inside our mind, not in the outer world or in our body, though they are popular scapegoats in false spiritual systems. Therefore a person cannot possibly get rid of evil until he has penetrated into his heart, into the center of his own being, and mastered the capacity to live and be centered there, to be established in that consciousness. How is it that the expression "source of evil" is used when the wise tell us that evil does not exist, but is only a corruption of the good? Notice that the Master does not say: "Get rid of evil," but "Get rid of the *source* of evil." In other words, evil in the form of negative thoughts or actions is a symptom of the presence of this thing.

What is this deadly thing? It is the consciousness of existence separate from God, which of course is a delusion for we are never separate from God who is our very Existence. Since God is All in All, we are ever one with him, the sense of separation being utterly false, a form of spiritual insanity. And that sense of separation is a primal delusion located at the center of our awareness like an obstruction in the eye that blocks or distorts the vision. As the Upanishad says: "He who thinks: 'I am one and God is another,' that man goes from death to death" (Brihadaranyaka Upanishad 4.4.19). That is, for such a one each birth is really a death. Then we begin to compound the evil by adding various definitions such as "I am a human being," "I am wise," "I am a sinner," and so forth. The ultimate madness manifests when we come to say: "I am God."

So the sense of separation from God, which results in the formation of the "I" concept, is the source of evil. Therefore, even if the "I" is killed or dissolved, if a consciousness or a conviction of separation persists, the "I" will grow back, just like a malignant tumor. Although all evil must be removed from us, it will be done in vain if the source of evil is not also gotten rid of.

There is also another secret of spiritual life here: if we go after the source right away, the process of eliminating evil will be relatively easy and painless, as well as quick. (I say *relatively*, please note.) However large the tree, if we go to the root we can kill it straightaway. Likewise, if we do not right away strike effectively at the root, the source, of evil, we shall be like someone trying to destroy a giant redwood tree by whittling away on it with a pocket knife. After years we might succeed, but how much better to cut off the root and accomplish the task much easier and faster. By striking at the source of evil we also avoid the danger of falling back into darkness and away from the spiritual path.

Another ploy of false religion is to convince us that we get rid of negativity by affirming or cultivating opposite qualities. But this is just shallow behavior modification and mind-gaming. We must fill our consciousness with the Divine Presence through meditation. We need not fight with evil impulses or thoughts, but instead ignore them and center our attention in the spirit-Self. Knowing all these things to be true, we must get busy and go deep within ourselves, to our very heart, our core or center. "Seek in the heart the source of evil and expunge it." You do not really kill it, because it does not even have a true existence of its own. But you simply end its darkness by invoking the Light.

It lives fruitfully in the heart of the devoted disciple as well as in the heart of the man of desire.

This is not a happy thought, but its truth is evident to anyone who observes both himself and others.

"It lives fruitfully." It extends itself, increases itself, and makes variations of its own theme. It is creative, projecting many manifestations of itself that exclude the vision of God from our heart. To eliminate these evils we must go into the heart and destroy the source rather than run around outside pursuing the symptoms. In this case, the mind and intellect are definitely outside elements, as well, and no amount of intellectual conditioning will have any real effect.

"It lives fruitfully in the heart of the devoted disciple as well as in the heart of the man of desire." This is extremely important, because we prefer to lie to ourselves and create a fine self-image for ourselves and others to believe in. Under that delusion we congratulate ourselves on not being like others when we are no better at all. Usually we are worse because of our pride.

One of the most damaging effects of false religion is its suppression rather than elimination of inner negativity. This is accomplished through the suppression of our perceptions or recognitions of our inner negativity. Many people live absolutely vile lives and have no idea that it is so–often just the opposite. False religion blinds its adherents to their true status.

I well remember the time when in my spiritual search I considered joining the Roman Catholic Church (this was in pre-Vatican II days). For some reason Protestants are traumatized by the idea of confession, and I was no exception. So one evening I began to think: If I went to confession now, what would I confess? And going back over the day I found a tremendous amount of sins to confess! This chagrined and frightened me, for I had not noticed any problems at all that day. I had been literally blinded to them. The next evening I did the same examination and found once again that my life was absolutely in tatters, spiritually speaking, when all the time I had been thinking that I was doing quite well as a yogi. Day after day when I examined my thoughts and deeds I found that I was profoundly spiritually sick, and even to some degree spiritually dead. Although I had shed the ignorant theology, the evil mindset was still present and thriving.

This is very much the situation with many people who believe they have extricated themselves from a false spiritual system. They have eliminated the superficial elements such as intellectual doctrines, but the spiritual distortion produced by the time spent in that system remains intact and continues to distort and often ruin their present endeavors. Highly dangerous are the instant conversions in the sense of drastic and instant behavior change, for such changes are usually pathological or ultimately non-existent. Testimonies of instant deliverance from long-standing problems sound good, for they appeal to our innate spiritual laziness. But the truth is that we ourselves must undo what we have done. We must dig ourselves out of the mire we have plunged into. We must take down stone by stone the structure of ignorance and evil which we have built through the aeons. And it takes will power and effort. Otherwise it is all untrue.

By overconfidence we become more susceptible to evil than by any other means. Usually the more "positive" we are in our thinking, the easier we are swept right into the garbage can along with all the rest. For this reason there is great truth in the adage: "Positive thinkers are positive stinkers." Of course, the positive thinking we are speaking of is self-delusion, not real positivity. The only way to think positive is to cultivate consciousness of God, the Only Positive.

"It lives fruitfully in the heart of the devoted disciple as well as in the heart of the man of desire." A bad, lax, or false disciple will never even come to discover this deadly Inner Dweller. Therefore the aphorism speaks of "the devoted disciple" since he alone can gain enough self-awareness to perceive his inner state and face up to it. As spiritual seekers we must realize that we are suffering from the same disease as everybody else. On a certain level there is no difference between us and the people we usually consider to be less than ourselves in evolution or spiritual aspiration and understanding, for the Master says that this source of evil is as fruitfully dwelling in our hearts as it is in theirs. This is extremely important, because few things are worse than this "pure" self-attitude that people can get just because they are working at spiritual development.

For us to look down on those who are not "spiritual" or religious is like people in a hospital priding themselves on the delusion that they are the well ones while everybody outside is sick. But they would not be in the hospital if they were not sick, would they? Simply registering in is a declaration of illness or defect. This is also why it is silly to blame religion when we see the faults of its adherents, for if they were not sick they would not need the therapy! The purpose of religion is healing, plain and simple. The sicker we are, the more medicine we take. In the same way, the more religious we are (in the true sense), the sicker we are acknowledging ourselves to be. So our religiosity is not a statement of health but of infirmity. By saying we are "on the path," we are admitting that we have not reached the Goal any more than those in the world around us.

We should not forget the Cheshire cat's words to Alice: If we were not mad we would not be here. The earth plane is the lowest and grossest level of existence that there is—even the astral hells are superior. So those who find themselves on the first rung of the ladder, and admit that they have been perched on it life after life, have no cause for boasting or looking askance at others.

Why does the source of evil live "fruitfully in the heart of the devoted disciple, as well as in the heart of the man of desire"? Because the sense of separate, even independent, existence arose in us the longer we began to manifest in relativity. As we passed through all the levels of evolution, that terrible thing was living and growing inside us, fed and increased by the world around us as we took it in and believed in it implicitly. As we evolve, so does the ego. (Here I mean evolution in the sense of the development of increased complexity and therefore capacity, not in the sense of growing closer to divinity.) Its manifestations become increasingly clever, and we become increasingly blinded. Evil, too, evolves so that we will not perceive its real nature. Indeed, we often admire evil for its ingenuity and power without realizing what it really is. However clever our intellect is, more so is our ego. However refined our state of consciousness may be, just so refined is our ignorance.

Material evil manifests as evil deeds. Mental evil manifests as evil thoughts. Spiritual evil manifests as evil religion. Such religion is the real "Satanism," beside which the antics of the minority that call themselves Satanists are quite insignificant. All the black magicians of the world have never equaled the evil and destruction perpetrated by the false "righteous" of all ages. The evolved person can become far more evil than the unevolved person. Of this we must be aware, for it applies to us. We who are more evolved than others are also (at least potentially) more spiritually sick than they are. So of what can we boast? We have no reason to feel ourselves superior to others just because our evil is more subtle and therefore less obvious. We have become genteel sinners, cultured demons.

The "man of desire" is one who is living solely for the fulfillment of his egoic desires and habits.

Only the strong can kill it out. The weak must wait for its growth, its fruition, its death. And it is a plant that lives and increases throughout the ages. It flowers when the man has accumulated unto himself innumerable existences. He who will enter upon the path of power must tear this thing out of his heart. And then the heart will bleed, and the whole life of the man seem to be utterly dissolved.

Is the refusal to do battle really the easy way out? Not at all. The next words are: "The weak must wait for its growth, its fruition, its death." In other words, the weak will have to wait until the inner evil disintegrates itself by its very nature.

So this is what will happen to the weak who will not engage in the struggle of the spirit. The evil will grow so much that it will ultimately destroy itself. But it will destroy them along with it. One of the most prevalent delusions of the "weak" is that they are not yet "ready" for conscious evolution, not quite "able" to commit themselves to the battle, but that if they wait a while things will get better and consequently easier. But they will not. Instead, evil will flourish and increasingly absorb the powers of the various bodies like a horrible parasite, eventually assimilating them totally unto itself. And they will indeed be incapable of spiritual life, but by then they will no longer even think about the subject.

I once met a frail woman who had an immense tumor attached to one side of her face. The tumor was larger than her head. As the tumor increased in size her body wasted away, until finally the body and the tumor both died. So it is with those who follow the negative path to its very end.

One of the worst and most beloved follies we can fall into is the idea that if we keep on feeding and fulfilling our desires they will in time fade away and we will be free. Just plain good sense should tell us that whatever is fed will grow and become even bigger and stronger. There are people who have so fed their lusts, giving up their vital life energies to satisfy the insatiable beasts, that they have correspondingly begun to fade away as the lusts became greater and more powerful. In time it is as though there is no real person left anymore, just a raging menagerie of material desires. This is true of any material drive that is given in to. In time the tiger we are riding will devour us. Of course such deluded people do not realize they are slaves, but think they are masters of their ravenous pets. But their fate will be that of the woman in a silly little ditty I learned as a child at camp:

> O she sailed away on a lovely summer's day
> On the back of a crocodile.
> "You see," said she, "he's as tame as he can be,
> "And I'll ride him down the Nile."
> So she waved her friends goodbye (as the crock winked his eye),
> Wearing a great big smile.

At the end of the ride, the lady was inside,
And the smile on the crocodile!

How many unpeople there are running frantically around seemingly fulfilling themselves, when in reality they are steadily melting away, consumed by the fires of their own desires. And the smile is on the face of the crocodile, for the Master does not say: "In time the weak will grow beyond evil and ignorance," but "the weak must wait for its growth, its fruition, its death." How long and how terrifying the prospect! For he continues: "And it is a plant that lives and increases throughout the ages." "It flowers when the man has accumulated unto himself innumerable existences." It is very flattering for someone to say to us: "You are an old soul," but the truth is, it is particularly in the "old soul" that this deadly thing is flowering. Once someone said to a man I knew: "You are a very old soul." To that he answered: "Then I must be a very dumb old soul if after so long I am still in this earth-plane kindergarten!"

"It flowers when the man has accumulated unto himself innumerable existences." In other words, when you and I have become aged, seasoned, and ripened, it is the strongest in us. The more evolved or developed we are, the more developed have ignorance and ego become simultaneously. I once heard a British psychiatrist telling how amazed he was in observing psychiatric work among "primitive" people. Instead of requiring years, even decades of psychoanalysis, these people were often cured after a twenty minute session. The "difficult" ones required two or three sessions—no more. This was because their egos were very simple. But those who have evolved to the point where conscious self-evolution is possible have greatly-developed egos with many convolutions and complexities. Sorry, but it happens to be one of the rules of the game. This is why we must truly become as little children to enter the kingdom of heaven (Matthew 18:1-3).

"He who will enter upon the path of power must tear this thing out of his heart." The expression "path of power" is used because the thing that destroys us is the idea: "I do this," "I do not do that," the root of which is "I do." Because we are identifying with the ego and the energy complex it draws around itself, the only power we can wield is that power. The path of power is also spoken of because the path to the Real is the path of mastery, the path of control of the lower self—not of others. Since our aspiration is for infinity, our goal is to wield the infinite power of God. But we have to chose: our life or God's life. If we stay centered in the ego, we will have nothing but its limited power.

Wise are those who through their failure realize that they need something more than their own power to succeed, and instead of turning to astral wanderers turn to God. If they can avoid or at least survive the false spiritual systems that abound, they have a good chance at succeeding in their quest. And the cornerstone of their success will be the realization that for their spirit to live their ego must die along with its illusion of separation from God.

We practice meditation to enable us to pass these various tests, both internal and external. What is essential is to be centered in our spirits, our consciousness, and detachedly observant of all that is external to us, including the levels of our being that we are used to thinking of as being inside us although they are as external to us as is the physical body. However, we cannot have that perspective until we have learned to transfer our awareness away from our wrappings and into our true nature as spirit. Which is why we meditate.

Having truly come to life inwardly, we are able to realize that what we formerly identified with as real and ourself is only the cosmic play of light and shadow, a dream that upon awakening will be no more. Thus we can say with full comprehension the words of the hymn: "Change and decay all around I see. O Thou Who changest not, abide with me." As a result we will not draw back in the times of dissolution and trial, but will steadily move onward, beyond the illusions that have so (literally) captivated us from life to life.

When we are practiced in ignoring all the noise and keeping intent on the Silence which is God, then when these things begin to melt away we will not mind. Through meditation we repolarize our life energies and our attention away from the dreams and press on toward our awakening. We unlearn falsehood and come to know the True.

The Master says that the whole life will seem to be utterly dissolved, but the man of wisdom, the man of meditation, will know that in actuality it is death that is being dissolved to make way for the advent of true life.

Let us look at those words again: "The whole heart will bleed and the whole life of the man seem to be utterly dissolved." Can we come in time to actively desire this, although others are pulling back in terror from the prospect? Of spiritual life it can be said just as it was about the Westward Movement in the last century: "The cowards never started and the weak died along the way."

Sometimes people say: "This is just what I have been looking for." And sometimes it is true, but although they have been seeking the gate it does not mean that they are prepared for what lies beyond it, or even for the effort that is required to open the gate and pass through. None of us has been looking for that, but it must be faced and undergone if we would succeed. Just as "eye hath not seen, nor ear heard, neither have entered into the heart of man, the things which God hath prepared for them that love him, (I Corinthians 2:9), so also the heart of man has not realized what is required for him to receive that free gift from the hand of God. Many love to seek but few can endure the finding: it is too real and demands too much change.

So we just love the anticipation and speculation as to what it might be like. But we do not expect God to play such a trick on us as to actually throw open the door, pull us through, shove us onto the path, and shout: "Run!" That we are not really expecting. Of course it is good that we do not know what is coming, for we might not seek for it!

This ordeal must be endured: it may come at the first step of the perilous ladder which leads to the path of life: it may not come until the last. But, O disciple, remember that it has to be endured, and fasten the energies of your soul upon the task. Live neither in the present nor the future, but in the eternal. This giant weed cannot flower there: this blot upon existence is wiped out by the very atmosphere of eternal thought.

Following the Path of Discipleship can be like riding a tiger: if we get off we will be eaten up. With this in mind the Master continues: "This ordeal must be endured." That word "endure" is not a very cheerful one, but it conveys the right idea: there is no escaping or mitigating the process. Just think of what gold goes through to be refined, or how much pressure and heat is exerted on a piece of coal for thousands of years before its blackness and opaqueness is changed into the clarity of diamond. That is why we say: "A diamond is a piece of coal that never gave up."

There is no avoiding the fires of the spiritual alchemy that turn us "from the unreal to the Real, from darkness to the Light, from death to Immortality." This is why Jesus would not take the drugged wine offered him before and during the crucifixion (Matthew 27:34). It was called "the wine of mercy," but he well knew that it was not merciful but deadening. And his eyes were not fixed upon the momentary sufferings of the cross but upon the resurrection and the infinite life that lay beyond it. We must have the same perspective.

Once we have started on the path there can be none of this frequently heard nonsense: "I am going to have to stop for a while and think it over." "I have to take 'time out' for a while and try to assimilate all that I've heard and learned." These are the words spoken by those who *never* continue in spiritual life. Such avoidance tactics are deadly for the aspiring disciple, who must be ever pressing forward and persevere: another word for endure.

This next statement is most important. "It may come at the first step of the perilous ladder which leads to the path of life: it may not come until the last." Some people go through the requisite ordeal at the very beginning. The higher Self of others knows they are weak, so it does not happen until they have progressed somewhat and become stronger and wiser.

Since we love comfort and ease we look upon the cataclysmic process as bad and ask: "Why do bad things happen to good people?" "Why do the good suffer so?" We do not realize that this is an essential process that is really merciful, for it frees them and readies them for higher consciousness. But this is why some people go along for a while and then become toppled by the advent of this ordeal. This may sound quite discouraging and not something to look forward to, but since the ordeal only takes place in relation to the unreal part of us, if our awareness is centered in our spirit we will not really find it so bad.

Let us back up for a consideration of the expression: "The perilous ladder which leads to the path of life." There are depictions in the Eastern Orthodox Church of the "Divine Ladder" which show people climbing up a ladder, at the top of which Jesus is waiting to receive them. When the top of the ladder is reached the work is done. But here the Master tells us that the ladder which we climb so laboriously is not itself the path to life, but what leads to the path of life. When we would like to think we are nearing the end we are really only nearing the beginning. Our struggle up the ladder is just the attempt to start.

The depictions of the Divine Ladder show people falling from the ladder (even being pulled from it by demons) and plunging downward into the mouth of a dragon. By this we see that the ladder is not just difficult and demanding, it is dangerous: perilous. It is dangerous because all the powers of evil inside and outside of us will do their utmost to stop us from getting up onto the path. This was the experience of Buddha long before us. There is a nineteenth century Protestant song that says: "Heaven wills to thee a crown. Hell is moved to cast thee down." But if we have shifted our consciousness into our higher selves, into "heaven," then all the antics and tactics of "hell" will be laughably ineffectual. The danger exists only insofar as we are caught in lower consciousness.

It is like a storm. If you are out in it, you will get wet and blown about, but if you are in a shelter, you will stay dry and calm. Therefore we hear much about taking refuge in God. It is all a matter of where we are in relation to the storm. If we insist on being of the earth, earthly, we shall then be blown about by every wind. If on the other hand we live and move in the spirit, we shall have peace. The danger and the pain is to the ego, never to the spirit. But if we identify with the ego it will drag us down into chaos along with it. If, however, we identify with the spirit we shall rise above all the storms.

The ladder is also perilous because failure may result in our having to wait for a long time before we can try the ascent again.

Of course all the perils come from inside us, which makes them all the more perilous since they are harder to cope with than outside influences because we usually identify with and foster them ignorantly.

"But, O disciple, remember that it has to be endured, and fasten the energies of your soul upon the task." Saint John Vianney said: "Go straight to God like a shot out of a cannon." The Upanishads say that the mind is like an arrow: aim it at the Goal and fly to God like an arrow.

"Therefore fasten the energies of your soul upon the task." This is why we have to follow the real path of power. We must control all our powers (energies) and focus them upon our spiritual work, which is the ending of the seeming separation between us and God.

To do this we must "Live neither in the present nor the future, but in the eternal." That is, we must let nothing in the present or future overpower us, but look at things with the eyes of eternity, with the eyes of spirit. We dare not say: "Today I cannot take up a dedicated spiritual life, but in the future I will." Rather, we must realize that it is the spirit alone that is and shall be, and lay hold on the realms of spirit now.

Notice that we are not told to live in eternity but in the Eternal. We are to live in God. For in God alone is freedom. Consider the fifteenth major arcanam of the Tarot, the "Devil" card. The two people in the foreground have chains around their necks and think they are enslaved to the Devil. But it is easy to see that they can slip off the chains without effort if they will just realize it. If we live in the present or future we will experience this false bondage, but if we slip the bonds and move our consciousness into the Eternal we shall know no bondage in any form.

Through false identities, through false bondage to "commitments," "relationships," and "obligations" we try to excuse ourselves from spiritual pursuit. Jesus spoke of this in his parable (Luke 14:16-24) in which the man invites his friends to a feast but they all make excuses not to come. One wants to try out plowing with his new oxen, another wants to go look at some property he has just bought, and another excuses himself because he has just gotten married. All of them, declares their prospective host, are unworthy of the feast.

In my earlier spiritual struggles when all I had was exoteric religion, I underwent a great deal of anguish. And one day I heard this song:

> So straight is the gate and so narrow
> The way to eternal day,
> And few are the pilgrims who find it,
> Too great is the price they must pay.
>
> Salvation is free, yet to gain it
> The soul must leave all things behind;
> Deny self and follow the Savior,
> The way straight and narrow to find.
>
> How rugged the path, yet God's glory
> Attendeth each soul on that way;

And brighter and brighter it shineth,
    Revealing a glad, perfect day.

But it's worth all it costs to be holy,
    It is worth all it costs to be true;
God's blessing and honor shall crown thee
    With power thy life to endue.

I knew it was the truth, and I never forgot it but resolved to "keep on keeping on."

We have but one true commitment, one true relationship and but one true obligation: to God. All else is the illusory bondage shown by the Devil card. That which obstructs spiritual life should not even exist for us on a practical level. In God, even karma does not exist.

"This giant weed cannot flower there." The sense of separation from God flourishes in time and space, in a consciousness "outside" of God. And what do weed flowers do? They make more seeds which become more weeds. In other words, the delusion of the separate, independent ego flowers and produces the seeds that will result in more delusions and more lifetimes. But in the Eternal that is not possible, for there all delusions and their seeds are roasted in the consuming fire that is God (Hebrews 12:29). So the process is simple: join yourself unto God in a perfect union and your karmas are dispelled like the morning mist. And that union is accomplished by meditation through which we cultivate the consciousness of God in which delusions cannot come to flower or seed.

In the eighth chapter of the Bhagavad Gita Sri Krishna says that there are two paths: the path of the moon and the path of the sun. The path of the moon leads to rebirth and the path of the sun leads to superhuman evolution. But the wise, He says, treads neither path but enters directly into the Being of God. "Free from greed, fear and anger, absorbed in me, holding fast to me, purified by knowledge-based tapasya, many have attained my state of being" (Bhagavad Gita 4:10). As in the child's game of tag, once we are "home" we are out of the game and free.

"This giant weed cannot flower there: this blot upon existence is wiped out by the very atmosphere of eternal thought." What is "eternal thought"? It is that thought which is the Eternal Itself, which is God. This is discovered only in the depths of meditation practice, and by its means the "giant weed" cannot grow, but in time is totally wiped out. In one sense we are transmuting ourselves into that "eternal thought." Just the atmosphere, just the radiation–that Light which blazes forth–dispels all ignorance. No evil, either inner or outer, can come near those who live in the Eternal Thought. (See *Soham Yoga, the Yoga of the Self*.)

5. Kill out all sense of separateness.

In case we might have missed the whole point, we come to Aphorism Five which is separated from Aphorism Four by all the material we have just considered. As has been said more than once, the sense of separateness is the primal evil, the root of all other evils, that nests in the very core of our being. It is the delusion that we are one thing and that God is another, that somehow we exist independently of God, different and separate, when all the time we are perfectly and irrevocably united to God so that we can legitimately be said to be gods within God. Reclaiming the awareness of that unity is the only true religion. Since he lived in that state consciously as a perfected yogi, a siddha, Jesus said: "I and my Father are one" (John 10:30), and "He who has seen Me has seen the Father" (John 14:9). And we shall one day be able to say the same things. That is our true destiny: to say as did Jesus, "the Father is in Me, and I in Him" (John 10:38). The mind cannot encompass it beforehand, but we shall inevitably attain it.

So it is important that we understand the nature of Krishna, Buddha, Jesus and other avatars, because if we do not understand their nature, their manifestation and their state of being, we cannot possibly comprehend our own destiny. Certainly, until we attain that status we shall not fully comprehend it, but even now there must be some conception of it, otherwise we shall not intelligently aspire to it. And without aspiration there is no attainment.

We have to consciously prepare ourselves to attain these higher states. If we deny these higher states, or do not even know they exist, they shall indeed not exist for us. Even though we do not fully understand, if we will at least give room in our minds to the possibility of these higher levels of consciousness we can begin to prepare for them. Of course the bedrock foundation of this believing and attaining is meditation.

One of the saddest truths is that most people's worship of God actually separates them from God, whereas it should link them with God. But when the concept, and consequently the approach, is wrong, then our attempts literally backfire on us, sending us in the opposite direction. The worship of God must be esoteric in nature, based on esoteric insight, and performed by those who have both esoteric knowledge and perception. Otherwise it is no worship at all, but a mockery both of us and of God. And the ultimate worship is meditation.

How shall we kill out all sense of separateness? By entering into our very depths and removing that primal illusion, the true original sin–keeping in mind that "sin" means to fall short of perception and apprehension. The primal (first) illusion is that of simply looking outward instead of inward. The moment that we turn from within and look outward we begin to see falsely.

Although it is the sense of separateness that the Master is speaking of in *Light On The Path*, it would not be amiss to say that externalized or outward-moving consciousness is really the primal evil. For through it we lose sight of God and therefore of our true selves and begin calling the separate illusion "myself."

So this whole sense of separateness has to be killed out thoroughly without reservation. And not through mere intellection or verbal philosophizing. The only way it can be done is by reestablishing within us the consiousness of identity with God. When we look at "ourselves," we see ourselves as utterly isolated and constantly changing entities. In other words, we can only see the falseness of ourselves, whereas God is the truth of ourselves. Therefore we must substitute the consciousness of God for the sense of separation. This is why we meditate, which keeps our eyes on God and fills us with divine consciousness. In God we will truly see ourselves. In "us" there is duality; in God there is non-duality.

6. Kill out desire for sensation.

When people spend much time in sense deprivation tanks they may experience great mental stress because they cannot stand just being aware of awareness. This is because they have been veiling their aware-ness for so many lifetimes by sensory stimuli that they are addicted to externalized consciousness.

"Kill out desire for sensation" means that we are to have no attraction for anything external. And we must remember that many things which we consider to be internal, such as emotions and intellect, are actually external to our consciousness even if they do seem to be within our bodies. Further, we must cut off desire for all subtle sensations: those that lie in the astral and causal realms as well as the obvious materi-al-physical sensations.

Notice that the Master does not say to cut off sensation, but to cut off desire or affinity for sensation. We need to learn to move among sensation without being affected or anyway conditioned by it. The wise have said that our external experiences must be to us like writing on water–without any internal effect or control. "Like the ocean, which becomes filled yet remains unmoved and stands still as the waters enter it, he whom all desires enter and who remains unmoved attains peace" (Bhagavad Gita 2:70).

Since they are external to us, even seemingly positive feelings, desires or emotions must have no influence or effect on us. Why? Because they are just feelings–they are not the real thing. Real peace, happiness, contentment, love, compassion and aspiration for spiritual life are indeed to be sought, but they are realities far beyond mere sensations. Most of them lie in the intelligence and will. Just as the ego is the false self, so the emotions and partially physical sensations that masquerade as these states are equally delusive and ultimately dissolve, leaving us desolate. This is a very difficult lesson for most of us to learn. But it must be learned if the real things are ever to be found by us.

We must especially avoid this kind of sensuality in spiritual life and not be drawn into desire for holy or exalted feelings when engaging in religious practices. The idea is to become utterly detached, indifferent to all sensations: to all that is outside of us. Or more exactly, to those experiences that will make us come to believe in the reality of externalities and will in time create in us the desire for such illusions, thus causing us to lose what is real and within.

We must continue to live, to reap our karmas, to fulfill our destinies–and it may require great effort to do so. But we must at the same time be easefully detached, viewing all that goes on as a great unfolding drama. There is nothing wrong in experiencing it just as long as we do not get drawn into it and drown our self-awareness within it through self-forgetfulness. Only the enlightened truly enjoy life. The rest are tossed about by alternating pleasures and pains, mistaking appearance for reality.

Like the dove of Noah we must not come to rest anywhere upon earth, but fly back to the Ark of divine being (Genesis 8:8-9). This is the higher meaning of Jesus' saying that he had nowhere to lay his head (Matthew 8:20). He could no longer center or confine his consciousness within anything in all the worlds, gross or subtle. There was nothing in which he could (or would) ground himself and with which he would establish an identity. "Our hearts are ever restless till they come to rest in Thee," wrote Saint Augustine, affirming that what is true of Christ is true also of us.

As mentioned before, there are fish in the sea that must keep moving or they will suffocate. We are such fish in the sea of evolving cosmic life. We must keep moving or we shall die to true consciousness and fall into the realm of death: of delusive consciousness that is no consciousness at all, practically speaking. "'Does the road wind uphill all the way?' 'Yes, to the very end.'" In many old stories there is great wisdom. For example, Red Riding Hood dawdled along the way picking flowers instead of getting on to her destination. So she entered into conversation with the wolf and ended up in his stomach. This is also true of the spiritual seeker. In the story of the tortoise and the hare we see that the hare lost because he kept stopping here and there while the turtle kept on moving steadily.

What we must destroy is the affinity for any relative state of consciousness or relative state of existence. And, again, the only way to do that is to keep pushing onward toward the Absolute.

The next rule is truly amazing, considering how we are constantly speaking of evolution.

7. Kill out the hunger for growth.

We are not told to kill out growth itself, for we came into this relative existence for that very purpose, but to kill out the hunger, the egoic impulse for the growth that is no true growth, the progress that is only the increase of the ego and not of the spirit-Self.

First we must come to the realization that we cannot become more than what we are. Therefore we must know our true nature. In a sense we do not need to grow, we need to discover and manifest. There is a great difference between the two verbs. Secondly, growth is an external experience and therefore an appearance only, not a reality. We cannot be anything but what we have always been. We can dig up an apple tree, take it around the world, fly it to many planets, and bring it back, and it will still be an apple tree, for that whole process was external to it.

There is story in South India about a bitter gourd who went to the holy city of Varanasi (Kashi), where every Hindu hopes to go at least once in his life. When Bitter Gourd came back, the animals and plants gathered around in admiration. "O Bitter Gourd!" they exclaimed, "just think, you have been to Kashi." "Yes," agreed the bitter gourd, "I have been to Kashi." "O Bitter Gourd," they asked, "did you worship Lord Vishwanath [Shiva] there in Kashi?" "Indeed," answered Bitter Gourd, "I worshipped Lord Vishwanath there." "Did you take your bath in the sacred Ganges?" "I certainly did take a bath in the Ganges." "Did you also worship Goddess Annapurna [the consort of Shiva] there?" "Yes, of course I did." "Then you came home." "Yes, I came home." "Bitter Gourd," they all said, "you must be a transformed person." "Yes, indeed, I can never be as I was," he declared. But then somebody thought to taste him, and found he was still bitter. Nothing external can create an internal change, although externals can and must facilitate the development of our internal awareness and evolution.

We are indeed to develop the ability to share in the infinity of God, but we will not grow into or become God. We will experience the being of God while remaining what we have always been. There will have been no essential change of being, but a total change of consciousness. This is so far beyond our present state that we simply cannot comprehend or conceive of it except to a minimal degree. But we can lay hold on it through yoga, for that and that alone is the true entering into the kingdom of God. The kingdom will always be God's, not ours, but by his loving will we can come to possess it in the sense of participating in it. For the kingdom of God *is* God.

But the ego wants to extend itself, to develop abilities that it can claim as its own, that will be under its own control. Such are the psychic and yoga powers which can become playgrounds for the ego and which the wise warn us to avoid assiduously, or at least approach only with great caution and spiritual preparation.

For every personal, natural ability there is a corresponding divine sharing which is bestowed upon us by God. For example, there is natural clairvoyance and there is divine clairvoyance. The source of one is materiality, though subtle, and the source of the other is infinite consciousness. It has also been observed that the two do not go together. This is why a viable spiritual system usually cuts off all natural psychic faculties and powers rather than developing them. This is a blow to the ego, but in time as the ego fades away the soul comes into its own and is illumined by God himself.

Our idea of growth, even on the physical level, is that of expansion, of pressing or moving outward and increasingly functioning in the external levels, whereas true spiritual growth is an expansion and increasing inwardly. Therefore the wise seeker reorients his focus from outward to inward. We do not attain outwardly: we enter into inward development.

Within us all there is the divine urge back to the Infinite, back to God alone. But the egoic impulse is: "I don't want to be just a human being, I want to be a god! I don't want to die, I want to live forever! I don't want to be unfulfilled, I want to be able to fulfill all my desires! I don't want to be helplessly controlled by the forces of nature, I want to myself master the forces of nature!" So when the deluded hear of the saints working miracles, they say: "I want to be a saint, too!" But they do not really want to be a saint, they only want to have power like the saints. There is a great difference. The foolish want to demonstrate great powers and have others call them "Master," but the wise wish to become Masters.

Let us repeat these short aphorisms to get an overview:

Kill out ambition.

Kill out desire of life.

Kill out desire of comfort.

Work as those work who are ambitious.

Kill out all sense of separateness.

Kill out desire for sensation.

Kill out the hunger for growth.

The Masters plainly present the truths that the hawkers in the contemporary metaphysical carnival would never dare to even speak if they knew them, which they do not. Why is this? Because the Masters are not part of the herd. They are never involved in movements and global endeavors, because they know that all spiritual progress is on a one-to-one basis.

8. Yet stand alone and isolated, because nothing that is embodied, nothing that is conscious of separation, nothing that is out of [outside] the eternal, can aid you. Learn from sensation and observe it, because only so can you commence the science of self-knowledge and plant your foot on the first step of the ladder. Grow as the flower grows, unconsciously, but eagerly anxious to open its soul to the air. So must you press forward to open your soul to the eternal. But it must be the eternal that draws forth your strength and beauty, not desire of growth. For in the one case you develop in the luxuriance of purity, in the other you harden by the forcible passion for personal stature.

Yet stand alone and isolated, because nothing that is embodied, nothing that is conscious of separation, nothing that is out of the eternal can aid you.

This is the real truth, the reason why in Sanskrit one of the words for salvation is *kaivalya*, which means literally, "one-aloneness." For those engaged in the Great Work there can be no support, anywhere, no dependency on anything outside themselves. All they can do is seek out their Source and return there. They cannot come to rest at any point in relative existence. And where will they seek their Source? Only

45

within. In the Gita we are told: "I am the Self abiding in the heart of all beings; I am the beginning, the middle and the end of all beings as well" (10:20). "This [Supreme Brahman] is… seated in the heart of all" (13:17). " [Brahman is] seated within the hearts of all" (15:15). "The Lord dwells in the hearts of all beings…. Fly unto him alone for refuge with your whole being. By that grace you shall attain supreme peace and the eternal abode" (18:61-62)."

So the Master says: "Stand alone." That is the only realistic view. We are always alone, separate in heart and mind, however surrounded we may be physically.

We have to be realistic about this aspect of spiritual life. If we lean on a crutch, when the crutch crumbles we will fall. When the world falls apart, then we will fall apart with it. Whatever external things we have an affinity for will ultimately fail us.

Think of the questing spirits as meteorites flying through the universe. They may have been doing so, unhindered, for incalculable ages, but if they come too close to the earth and are drawn into its atmosphere, they are incinerated or else reduced to only a token of their original size and fall to earth, stopped in their flight. Therefore we must keep our distance from all that "is," but in reality is not.

"Yet stand alone and isolated, because nothing that is embodied,… can aid you." There is no physical entity that can be our help. Why? Because embodiment is the result of ignorance. This is why when Pythagoras' students wanted to celebrate his birthday, he refused, saying: "The day of my birth is my shame. For if I had been a man of true knowledge I would not have needed to be born here on earth."

This world in which we find ourself is the least and lowest in consciousness: in evolution. It is actually lower than the astral hells, because there the mind is much more awake and insightful as to why it has come there, whereas upon earth we are usually completely unaware as to the why of our incarnation here. In the astral hells we remember all the lives that have resulted in our ending up there, but upon the earth we usually do not even remember that we have had any previous existence at all. The astral hells are very meaningful to the people in them, but here on earth people understand nothing about themselves or it, including why they are here.

Nothing embodied can help us because embodiment is a veiling rather than a revealing. Therefore that which is embodied is that which is covered and hidden. That is, the consciousness is confined to the body instead of centered in itself. Externalized consciousness compared to internalized consciousness is what fool's gold is to real gold. We are truly lost. And only when we "come to ourselves" can there even be the possibility of our being saved or found.

Instead of being in our Self as we should be and working and evolving through conscious use of our vehicles of body, mind, etc., we are drawn out into the vehicles and lose ourselves in total awareness of them. We are like the hero in the old western films: when the stagecoach horses run away the man jumps into the middle of them and holds on, hoping to stop them. That is our situation exactly. We are no longer controlling and driving in an intelligent way, but have thrown ourselves right into the pounding hooves. And most of us get flattened by them from life to life. Instead of being masters of the bodies, the bodies are the masters of us.

By these few words the Master is telling us that all power is within us, not outside us. "Nothing that is conscious of separation... can aid you." That includes our own egoic mind and intellect, what to speak of other people. Another person bound like us, drowning like us, can hardly save us.

Also, one of the favorite excuses to avoid spiritual life is to tell how "let down" or "hurt" or "disappointed" we have been in others who were supposedly spiritual. This is shameful and spineless silliness. How often we hear people saying: "I used to: go to the church/temple/ashram/ center/meditation, and they hurt me... they let me down... I became disillusioned," etc., etc., etc. Such people never sought God. They sought a group of people in which they could be one of the herd, or perhaps eventually a leader of the herd. They sought for a group identity, a place of mutual ego support.

The antidote to this and all other delusions is to fix our minds on God. Then we will not be let down or hurt. Considering how from life to life our own egos, minds, intellects and bodies have done nothing but hurt and let us down, it is high time to separate from them and take refuge in the spirit!

Beware of "helpers"! There are many people whose egotism manifests in a deluded concept of themselves as teachers and uplifters of humanity. They wander around thrusting their supposed wisdom and assistance on whatever victims they can find. Many of them do great harm to those they "help." Who, then, can help us? Only those who see the divine unity in all things can help us. And I mean those who really do see the divine unity, not those who only believe in or talk about it.

When a candle is lighted, other candles can be lit from it. Fire communicates fire. In the same way divine consciousness communicates itself from consciousness to consciousness. During my spiritual meanderings, especially in India, I met various grades of spiritual teachers. Many of them were advanced yogis whose auras were expanded far beyond their bodies. When I came into their presence I felt subtle currents flowing all around me. In the presence of some of them I felt great upliftment. But in the presence of all of them there was a common flaw: I was made keenly aware of them, but forgetful of myself. It was also evident that their consciousness was of a duality: themselves and those around them. Because of this, there was a desire on their part to effect a change in those around them. This desire was in some of them noble and benevolent, but still based on a sense of separation, of duality.

Swami Sivananda of Rishikesh was in another league altogether. He was established in perfect unity with God, and therefore in perfect unity with those around him. Whenever I entered his presence his self-illumination communicated itself to me, and instead of being drawn out of myself in admiration of him, I found myself becoming intensely self-aware. In his presence I found my own consciousness changed. Rather than being transformed into a groupie I found myself strengthened in my endeavors for self-knowledge and spiritual freedom. Because of his unified vision, he saw the reality within us and "spoke" to that.

The sun does not need to think about giving light or heat. Its nature is to do so. In the same way those who are truly perfected in divine consciousness remain so in unbroken communion with the Infinite, never taking their eyes away from the One. Even when they move and speak with us they are doing so in that perfect consciousness, beholding us as we truly are: in God and of God. Since that vision is the only true one, it communicates itself to us in a mysterious way beyond intellect or emotion.

Many think that they would like to meet and even live with the masters but it is not always so pleasant an experience, for the masters, being themselves free from ego and knowing the ego as the anti-self within, do not deal with us on the egoic level, but only on the spiritual plane. Most people who seek out "the masters" have unfulfilled egos, especially spiritual egos which are the worst of all, which they expect those masters to soothe and please. Even though they know the ego must go, they usually want the masters to give their ego the equivalent of a nice long "last meal of the condemned," and then easily and painlessly dissolve their ego without their even knowing it or feeling it—or even being changed by it! This of course is an absolute impossibility, being contrary to the nature of things, including that of the ego.

The masters will not placate or coddle our egos. Rather, they either ignore their demands or they ruthlessly go after them to rout them and destroy them. But this can only be done with our cooperation. To assist at one's own surgery without anesthesia is not an easy thing. But if we would gain benefit from association with the masters that is exactly what must be done. Otherwise we will only turn away from the masters in indignation accusing them of being without love or understanding–even of being egotistical!

Many of the spiritually diseased have an obsessive insistence that saints and masters should be childlike. What they really want is for them to be too naive to see through their ego-gaming. They have forgotten how devastatingly insightful and candid children can be. The masters cannot be coerced into playing the little mind-games at which we excel. They will not play house with our egos and agree to be our Mommy, our Daddy, our Baby or (worst of all) our Lover. They will be the best and truest friends that our immortal spirits can ever have. But to be that, they will have to also be the most implacable enemies that our egos can ever have. So if we identify with our spirit we will call them friend, but if we identify with our ego we will call them enemy.

Regarding his guru, Swami Sriyukteswar Giri, Yogananda wrote in his autobiography: "Students came, and generally went. Those who craved a path of oily sympathy and comfortable recognitions did not find it at the hermitage. Master offered shelter and shepherding for the aeons, but many disciples miserly demanded ego-balm as well. They departed, preferring life's countless humiliations before any humility. Master's blazing rays, the open penetrating sunshine of his wisdom, were too powerful for their spiritual sickness. They sought some lesser teacher who, shading them with flattery, permitted the fitful sleep of ignorance."

The masters only love God. Therefore they only love the God in us. The rest is nothing to them, though they will help us to get rid of all in us that is not God, because those things destroy us by making us forget our real nature. Even the company of saints and angels would be detrimental to us if it made us forget what we really are. Such is the knowledge of the masters, and since they love us in God they will not settle for giving us anything but the best they have to give: freedom from ego and all that goes along with it.

But we cannot become dependent even on the masters, for they cannot "do it" for us, but can only point out the way. The masters despise such dependency as being detrimental to us, knowing that our spiritual evolution is exclusively between us and God. Because of this, *Light On The Path* is exhorting us to never place our trust or hope in anything outside ourselves. Instead, we are to base our spiritual quest on that which is within, where there is divine unity, because "nothing that is out of the eternal can aid you."

Learn from sensation and observe it, because only so can you commence the science of self-knowledge.

By "sensation" is meant any perception that enters our consciousness, whether physical, emotional, intellectual or spiritual. Thoughts and movements of the will are sensations just as much as the messages of the physical senses. We are told to put our minds on God and to ignore all else. Now we are being told to observe and learn from sensations which are external to us. But this is not a contradiction, for we are not to immerse ourselves in sensations, but only to objectively observe them. This is accomplished through keeping our consciousness centered in the spirit. That is, we center ourselves in pure awareness and observe the sensations that are arising. It is not inappropriate to say that we use our awareness as a kind of lens through which we focus on external phenomena. It is a divine eye through which we perceive what is outside us. But through it we always remain inside and safe. Since even our perceptions of externals are really interior experiences of the modifications of the energy field of the mind, we can come to comprehend the ways of our mind through observation. Once we do this we shall no longer be fooled by its tricky ploys. We must learn to interpret what arises around us in the motion picture of life.

51

Since all that happens to us is an echoing back of forces set in motion by us in the past, it should be evident that the present reveals the character of our past, and therefore of our mind and will. For all actions require thought and will as their basis. Though we think we are seeing the world, we are really seeing our own psychic face. The world is like a musical instrument; what we hear is what we ourselves are producing. When Buddha, and later Jesus, taught that we should do to others the things we would have done to us, they were stating a fact of life, the principle of karma. What we do to others shall be done in turn to us. So what is being done to us now is what we have done to others in the past. If we do not like it, we have no one to blame but ourselves. Although others may be the instruments of our karmic manifestation, in reality everything that is done to us is really being done by us to ourselves. We are slapped only because we have slapped in the past and now that seed is coming to fruition as a slap in the present. We are wronged only because we have wronged others. If we do not like our present, then we must watch what we are doing now and see that we do not keep sowing the seeds whose fruits we do not like.

There is no one to blame but ourselves regarding whatever happens to us. It is a bitter pill to accept full responsibility for our lives and deeds, but it must be done if we would intelligently progress in any aspect of life. How often we hear people blaming environment, parents or peers for their problems and their "hurts." But that is self-deception. We alone are the ones to indict.

If then we will carefully observe and analyze our daily experiences, both internal and external, we can come to some intelligent diagnosis of where we are spiritually. The world around us is a play, but we are the authors, and our minds and intentions are revealed as it unfolds. Clear-sighted understanding of our surroundings will result in understanding of ourselves. Our minds must be carefully observed since they may be the instruments of the lying ego. We need not believe our minds, but we must observe them. Our minds are often liars, but behind the lies is the truth. We must learn to interpret the mind and its antics, not necessarily accept or believe them. When we can do this, the mind, like the world, will become a conveyer of truth to us, even though indirectly.

The world is ultimately not real. Anyone can say that, but to perceive it is quite another matter altogether. Silk flowers can look absolutely real, but close scrutiny shows otherwise. Similarly, by watching the world carefully we will come to see both what it is and what it is not. The Master says to observe and learn, not give in to it, believe it, accept it and be pushed around by it. This is also true of the internal world, especially the world of mind and emotion. In the Yoga Sutras of Patanjali, one of the essential requisites for successful spiritual life is swadhyaya, which means self (swa) study (adhyaya). Here the word "self" refers to the wrappings of the spirit, not the spirit itself. The most important of the wrappers is the mind. If we study it, as well as our emotions, etc., we will see their natural folly and illusory character. More to the point, we need to realize their frequent treachery and unreliability.

Our ego, mind, emotions, intellect and desires are often our implacable enemies. Jesus had this in mind when He said: "A man's enemies will be those of his own household" (Matthew 10:36). For some people, because of their karma, their earthly family or friends may be inimical to their spiritual progress. But in the more psychological sense that our "household" consists of our own inner faculties, it is usually true for everyone. Our bodies, emotions, senses, intellect and desires can militate against our progress and with fiendish genius expend themselves in endeavors to ruin our spiritual life. Now, they have no objection to fake religious or spiritual life, they will even push us toward it. But they shall literally war to the death against our true spiritual progress. We must see through them and know them for what they are and what they are not. For our inner household is the hardest army of all to resist and conquer.

So must you press forward to open your soul to the eternal. But it must be the eternal that draws forth your strength and beauty, not desire of growth. For in the one case you develop in the luxuriance of purity, in the other you harden by the forcible passion for personal stature.

We must not misunderstand: in their usual unpurified state our body, emotions, mind, intellect and will cannot be opened to the eternal, for they are themselves presently bars to our attainment of the eternal. When purified and elevated they can be instruments for our growth into the eternal, but they will be left behind at the gates of eternity. As the Upanishads say, God is that from which the mind and the senses turn back. They can only go so far, and then no more. In the presence of the eternal the senses fade away and are transcended. Therefore our process of meditation need cannot involve these things which will ultimately be turned away from the door of God. From the beginning our meditation is formless, without concept, without intellection, focused on the pure consciousness within. (Again, see *Soham Yoga, the Yoga of the Self.*)

We must press forward to open our spirits to the eternal because we have become enclosed, locked in the various energy bodies. The simile is often given of sea water that is separated from the sea by being enclosed in bottles. Although the separation may last for aeons, the moment the bottle is opened or broken the water within will regain its unity with the greater body of water. The bottled water is the individual spirit and the sea is the Infinite Spirit, God. After ages of confinement we now want to break these jars and let our consciousness participate in the life of infinity.

Our spirits can be opened to the eternal alone, to nothing else. One purpose of our energy body-bottles is to keep the spirit untouched by the temporal state of existence. The spirit is ever-virgin, betrothed to God alone, and within this virgin spirit, finite though it be, the infinite consciousness can be enclosed and experienced as its very own.

We cause confusion and suffering for ourselves by trying to open our spirits to things other than God. We are trying to get our spirits to rest where there is no rest, for the eternal alone is the destiny of the spirit. "But it must be the eternal that draws forth," declares the Master. Although we say that the plant breaks through the earth, we can equally say that the sun draws it from the earth. So "it must be the eternal that draws forth your strength and beauty, not desire of growth."

Only the eternal, then, can produce spiritual life. As plants are made to grow by the light and heat of the sun, so by continually centering our awareness in consciousness, in spirit, through meditation, we are drawn upwards. It is both an action by us and an action upon us. In *Cyrano de Bergerac*, Cyrano tells a man that he has flown to the moon by standing on an iron disk and throwing a magnet out in front of the disk. The magnet would then draw the disk to itself. By repeatedly tossing the magnet ahead of the disk he was able to propel himself to the moon. Absurd as it might be in *Cyrano*, that is what we are doing in meditation. We are entering into spirit-consciousness, and that alone is acting upon us.

We should note that the Master says that it is the eternal which we must use. This informs us that the eternal can be an object. "For in the one case you develop in the luxuriance of purity." That is, the divine, which is all-pure, all light, and stainless, develops into this abundance of inner presence, which we produce through meditation. However, "in the other you harden by the forcible passion for personal stature."

Through the one we want to share in the divine infinity so we can love God infinitely. The spirit wants to receive, to give back. The spirit of course rejoices in God, but wishes to become perfect so God can rejoice in it. The spirit wishes to become a flawless mirror in which God can behold His own beauty.

What, then, is the purpose of finding God? What is it that the spirit truly desires? The fundamental urge of the spirit is to give itself as an offering unto and into God, to merge with God. The spirit knows that it is the drop and that God is the ocean.

When we feel an aspiration to know God we must first discover the source of the aspiration, for the ego can aspire to godhood just as the spirit can. This is why Sri Ramana Maharshi used to continually challenge seekers to discover who was doing the seeking. The ego would like to know God in hope of gaining for itself the powers and glory of God.

All the evils done in the name of religion are continually being pointed out by those who hope to thereby excuse themselves from following a legitimate spiritual path which involves humility and obedience: both deadly poisons to the ego. But what they (willingly) do not realize is that religion is of two kinds: ego-motivated and spirit-motivated. The fruits of the two will be utterly different. This is why in religion we have to be very careful and inquire of ourselves: "Who is being religious? Who is 'on the path'? Who is it that is seeking God?" In most people it is the ego itself that is seeking. But since it would be dissolved if it really came into contact with God, it veers off and creates a false path and a false god. Alternately, it rebels or gives up, and falls back. Only the spirit can go all the way to God.

In the very beginning of our spiritual search we should ask ourselves: "Do my seemingly spiritual impulses come from me, my spirit, or do they come from my ego?" The Master also points out that if our seeking comes from the ego it will cause us to be locked even more into our egoity, reducing our spiritual pursuit to just another passion. This is why supposedly religious people hate and harm one another, going into hysteria at any disagreement with their ideas and ways, striking out at "heresy" and "heretics." Or they may simply run away the moment they hear something they do not like or agree with, and try to block the offending idea or individual out of their minds. This latter is the more mellow reaction of New Age egos.

Those whose religious involvement comes from the spirit are aware that intellectual concepts count for very little, in fact they know that any philosophical concept is imperfect and never a statement of absolute truth. Further, they know that true spiritual life manifests as a result of evolution, never from intellectual conviction. Therefore no outside influence should be brought to bear on another's spiritual life. The true spiritual seeker must always be independent and free. Although discipline and even obedience are essential in spiritual life, they must be voluntary, never imposed. They must arise from within.

Those who are dominated by the ego say: "Never bring into my world something I do not like or approve of." Naturally, they consider God to be just like them and project the same egoic motivations and reactions onto him. They then define sin as something that angers or offends God: a thing is sinful simply because God dislikes it. The realization that sin and virtue are only in relation to what keeps us away from God and what aids us in reaching him is simply beyond them since they can only impute selfish attitudes and motives to God. They cannot understand that neither our sin nor our virtue mean anything to God because they are only momentary appearances. "The Omnipresent takes note of neither demerit nor merit" (Bhagavad Gita 5:15). Nor can they really believe that God never changes in either His relationship to us or His attitude toward us. And the realization that God never deals with us on the egoic level is simply too devastating for them to even consider, much less accept.

9. Desire only that which is within you.

That which is real, which is infinite, is within; that which is finite, is false and illusory, is outside. In truth we can never see that which is outside, but only what is inside: the interpretation of the perceptions of the senses. So we should seek only that which is within, for God himself is within us as the Life of our life, the Spirit of our spirit.

10. Desire only that which is beyond you.

A basic flaw of our present status is the desire to dig in and stay in one spot, mistaking this for peace and security. Since this is not really possible, we either deceive ourselves or actively suffer. We must keep pressing ever onward, never content with the attainment of the moment. In spiritual life we need to be like Rockefeller. When he was asked how much money it would take to satisfy him, he replied: "Just a little more." We must never be satisfied with anything less than the Absolute.

Sri Ramakrishna often told of the woodcutter who was told by a wandering monk: "Go on further into the forest." He did so, and found a deposit of iron ore. At first he was elated, planning how to mine it, but then he remembered that the monk had said to go on, not just to find something and stop. So he went further and found a copper mine. Keeping on, he found a silver mine, a gold mine, and finally a place with many gems in the earth. All this he gained because he did not stop moving on.

Instead of being like little Jack Homer with the plum on his thumb, we must keep asking: "What next? What more?" There is a divine greed, a divine ambition, and we must cultivate it. We are capable of possessing all the worlds from lowest to highest but still there will remain something more. There is That which lies beyond all worlds, beyond all that "is" in a relative sense. Nevertheless it can be attained by those who apply themselves wholeheartedly.

The emanation of all the worlds occurs in cycles of projection and withdrawal. Why is this? Why has not the realm of relativity been once sent forth and maintained eternally? The cyclic process is necessary because the individual consciousnesses get caught in the higher states of being. Since there is no suffering there, and since those realms are endlessly fascinating, it is possible for those who evolve to those states to delay their progress in exploration of the seemingly infinite possibilities accessible to them. Therefore even those worlds must be periodically dissolved in order to remind them of their higher Goal, to unsettle them and stimulate them to move onward.

God meditates on us, and we meditate on Him, and in time the two become One. God seeks us, and we seek Him, and at last we "find" one another. God in us, and we in Him—our ultimate unity is inevitable. It is because God seeks us that we seek Him. He having chosen us, we choose him. Therefore the questing spirit should never doubt or despair. Our search for him is but a mirroring of His search for us. And God never fails in His intentions. The entire universe has but one purpose: our return to God.

11. Desire only that which is unattainable.

This has really already been covered. We can attain evolution through all the worlds, but we cannot attain the status of the infinite God. However, we can so purify and evolve ourselves that we become capable of sharing in the Infinite Consciousness, in that way attaining the unattainable. And that alone is worthy of being desired by us.

We need to stop and take another look at the three admonitions: "Desire only that which is within you. Desire only that which is beyond you. Desire only that which is unattainable." Although they may sound like word puzzles, they hold a very serious meaning that is the key to success in sustaining spiritual endeavor.

12. For within you is the light of the world—the only light that can be shed upon the Path. If you are unable to perceive it within you, it is useless to look for it elsewhere. It is beyond you; because when you reach it you have lost yourself. It is unattainable, because it for ever recedes. You will enter the light, but you will never touch the flame.

For within you is the light of the world—the only light that can be shed upon the Path.

Within us is this Divine Light—we are ourselves the light of the world. As Jesus said: "Ye are the light of the world" (Matthew 5:14). In us alone is the means to see our way out of darkness. If we look outside, we will find only delusive darkness, even though it is a mere appearance and nothing more. And if we live and walk in that outer darkness, we shall stumble and fall. It is inevitable. But if we live inside, centering our awareness within, then we and our path will be illumined, for there is no other light possible in this or any other world.

In Sanskrit the state of enlightenment is called *swayamprakash*–self-illumined, for the spirit, the true Self, is Light. The light of the world is not in the world at all! It is in us. We must realize and experience this if we would not live in darkness. This inner light is in truth "the only light that can be shed upon the Path."

It is only natural that as intellectually developed beings we should enjoy hearing and reading about spiritual subjects. This does help in our spiritual quest. But when it comes to real evolution, which is the walking of the Path, then we must rely upon the inner light alone. If we attempt to live our spiritual life solely through the intellect we will become hopelessly entangled. This is especially true since spiritual realities lie mostly outside the scope of the intellect and therefore often appear absurd or contradictory within its context.

Also, if we are not careful we will substitute intellectualization about spiritual life for spiritual life itself. This is especially true in the West. There is a parable about a group of "seekers" who were confronted by two paths. Each had a sign and an arrow pointing along it. One sign said: "The way to God." The other said: "The way to a discussion about God." Everybody went to the discussion! This is what happens when we become so acclimatized to the cage of the intellect that we are like the imprisoned bird that is afraid to venture beyond its bars.

We can "reason" ourselves out of and into just about anything except spiritual life. When it comes to that, we must utilize the inner light of our spiritual consciousness. That alone reveals the path. Therefore we must not fall into the dangerous practice of mind-gaming, for many people mind-game themselves right out of spiritual life. "Since we are all God right now, what is the need to do anything?" is one of the favorite exit lines.

Most importantly, another person's light cannot illumine our path. Once a man went to consult a saint, and when leaving asked him to pray for him. The saint replied: "No. I cannot eat for you, or breathe for you, and neither can I pray for you. That you must do for yourself."

We can see only through our own eyes, not those of another. Only false teachers try to impose on us their vision of things, to make us see as they see. True teachers give us the means to open our own inner vision and see for ourselves. They may tell us how they see a thing, but never with the idea of making us see it in the same way. Also, if we come to realize that our view is imperfect or incorrect, we must set about correcting it ourselves.

There is an account of a Zen master who always taught: The Buddha Is The Mind. But one day he called a monk and told him to go to a disciple who was living far away as a hermit and tell him that he now understood differently: No Buddha, No Mind. So the monk hastened away and told the hermit about the new understanding. "Well," said the hermit, "I still say The Buddha is the Mind." Back rushed the monk to "tell on" him. But when he relayed the incident the master smiled happily and said: "I see he has gained maturity." He had integrity, too.

There is no place in spiritual life for an unquestioning cult-slave mentality. But this occurs in Eastern religion just as much as in Western religion, the difference being that in the East they are not as coercive, hostile, and threatening. One time I heard an American ask his guru: "What do we believe about that?" How absurd! He obviously did not believe anything about the question, so "we" did not believe anything at all. There is nothing wrong in asking what a person's belief is, or what a scripture teaches, but to ask with the intention to unthinkingly accept whatever will be said is a crime against ourselves and truth.

We must light up the inner light. We must be like the Hermit of the Ninth Major Arcanum of the Tarot in the Waite deck. He is holding aloft the lamp in which shines the six-pointed star, the symbol of the union of human and divine consciousness. Yet, the Hermit does not peer outward into the darkness, but stands with bowed head and closed eyes, his consciousness turned within. He is seeing with the inner light which the outer lamp symbolizes.

If you are unable to perceive it within you, it is useless to look for it elsewhere.

If in the beginning we cannot perceive the Light, we keep on looking within through meditation, where everything is present. All illumination is there, although we are not perceiving it. When we go from the light into a darkened room, or into the light from a dark place, at first we cannot see anything. But gradually our eyes adjust and we see everything. So in time we will see all. Our inner eye needs adjustment, attunement, and healing from what is called in Sanskrit *ajnana tamira*, the glaucoma of ignorance. Also, the cataracts of illusion and material consciousness must be removed before we can see truly. And sometimes we do not see because we are not really looking at all, or are looking in the wrong place.

It is beyond you; because when you reach it you have lost yourself.

"You" and "yourself" do not refer to the true Self, our immortal spirit, but to the false ego that has usurped the place of the true "us," or produced in us the erroneous experience of our true Self as separate from God. Here, too, is a clue as to why we may be seeing only darkness when we look for the light. We may be looking through the eyes of our blind egos which are incapable of seeing the light. There is no adjustment or healing for the ego: it must go. Also, we may be looking at the ego itself, which is the quintessence of darkness.

When the sun is in the sky many objects shine, even blindingly. But when the sun sets, there is only darkness, for in those objects there is no light. Even though the body, emotions, mind, intellect, etc., can reflect the light of life, it is a mistake to seek for that light in them. Our spirits are the suns that lend temporary illumination to the lesser parts of our present being, parts that in time shall be discarded for higher consciousness. Therefore we must cultivate spiritual consciousness.

We seek God because God is drawing us to Himself. We, being egotistical, attribute that action to ourselves and say: "Oh, I am seeking God," whereas in reality we are just answering the call. The classical Sanskrit definition of meditation is: "The unceasing flow of the mind toward God." When we get beyond ourselves (or, more accurately, our unselves), then we will reach the Light. It will do no good just to complain that we do not see the light. We must get out of the darkness of our ignorance and ego, and into the light. Then there will be a possibility of seeing. The senses, mind, and intellect have never seen God, nor can they. But when we go beyond them we shall find our spirits; and there, one with them, shall we successfully seek God. When we find ourselves we find God, for he is one with us. There is an eternal unity and an eternal duality. Meditation takes us out of the little false "I" and establishes us in the consciousness of God. And in that consciousness we come to know ourselves in God through Divine Knowing.

It is unattainable, because it for ever recedes. You will enter the light, but you will never touch the flame.

This is because our "hands," the body vehicles with which we would touch or which would act as an intermediary for some kind of contact, will have long ago been transcended. We will have entered into and become the light, therefore it will never be an object. We will behold and possess it within, never outside.

"It is unattainable because it for ever recedes." We can get the false light right away through a little bit of some psychic exercise, and congratulate ourselves on our exalted state. But that is the lying light. The true light keeps saying: "Take a step more; come on a little further." If we are ego-centered we may become frustrated and angry at the divine elusiveness. But if we keep following its drawing of us, the further it draws us the more the veils of illusion will drop away. Then at last there will be no more veils, only the Light. What, then, will be left to lay hold on it? For we shall have entered into and become one with It.

There is no place in this for the ego, which cannot by its very nature ascend to that status. In the ego-oriented systems there is much talk about the descent of higher consciousness. This is indeed true, but such descents mean nothing unless they motivate us to ascend to the Source, which alone is salvation. We go higher and higher until the distinctions of higher and lower are left far behind along with the "who" that was ascending. What will then remain? That which has always been there: the pure spirit.

The descent into matter and our subsequent evolution is really only a matter of ideation. It is impossible for us to "go" anywhere since space and time are only appearances, not realities. But we have fallen into the ideational exercise and come to believe that it is really "going on" and that we have fallen away from God in a spatial sense.

Consider how it is when we watch a motion picture, a television story, or a play in a theatre. Willingly we lay aside our knowledge that it is all false, merely a pretence, and begin reacting to what we see. We become amused, afraid, anxious, indignant, happy, relieved, disgusted, etc., moving through a spectrum of reactions triggered off by what we are observing. Though knowing it is fantasy, we willingly respond to it as reality. All of creation, from highest to lowest, is but a projection of consciousness, a dream of the Infinite. Yet we have allowed ourselves to become convinced of its reality and become drawn right into the midst of it, no longer able to draw back and see it as it is and as it is not.

"You will enter the light, but you will never touch the flame." This is because God in his essential nature is never experienced as an object, only as the eternal Subject of which we are an eternal part. So we experience ourselves as within God, and God as within us. This is the eternal Unity that is the sole Reality of our existence.

13. Desire power ardently.

The Path of Power has already been referred to. The next directive, then, is: "Desire power ardently." What is the power we should seek? The power of mastery of the lower self and its illusions, the inner power to seek God. What is wanted is the power to run unhindered to the Goal, to intensify our efforts. Because of this, we then begin to increase and conserve our personal power by means of various disciplines in thought and deed. It is here that the observance of the "ten commandments of yoga," yama and niyama, is so important.

We also begin to simplify our life so we can direct all our activity toward finding God. It is not external power we need, but internal power, for it is the inner power that impels us onward, toward the Light. We must seek inner empowerment to develop the requisite tenacity of will, for much, if not all, lies in the will. On every level we strive to become more and more self-contained so we can gather the power to impel ourselves into the Infinite.

Though it may not seem so at first sight, self-respect and integrity are also part of this conservation of power. If we look around us we will see that many people who profess high ideals readily lay aside those ideals if sufficient reward or punishment is placed before them. This is why the Stoic philosopher Epictetus (whose *Discourses* are of great value for the seeker) challenged his hearers to consider at what price they would sell their choice and will. Then, having discovered what they would sell out for, they should strive to become indifferent to it so they would never sell themselves for any reason, whether gain or loss.

We are to desire this power ardently: flamingly. This desire will consume all that which opposes it, so the person will be single in will and act. In a sense, it must consume us, but it is the fire in which the phoenix of the immortal spirit is manifested. Instead of death, it brings us life.

Part of Hindu worship consists of offering burning camphor. This is because camphor burns without leaving a residue—is totally consumed. So also in our desire all must be consumed except that which is the object of our desire. The energies of our bodies, gross and subtle, are consumed in the race for the infinite. This being so, only those who are willing to be so consumed should begin the race. Nothing can be held back: that fire consumes all. That is why Jesus warns us: "Whoever seeks to save his life will lose it, and whoever loses his life will preserve it" (Luke 17:33).

14. Desire peace fervently.

How can there be peace? By moving the center of our consciousness from the realm of continual change that is this world and directing it toward that everlasting Self as its goal. Just as a cease-fire is not a real peace, so true inner peace is not the simple cessation of agitation or change, but the ending of the *possibility* of agitation and change. It is achieved by going beyond all that is capable of change. That alone is peace. Deafness should not be mistaken for silence. The peace spoken of here is not a mere non-experiencing of any pain or agitation, it is being established in that state where pain and agitation simply do not exist.

15. Desire possessions above all.

16. But those possessions must belong to the pure spirit only, and be possessed therefore by all pure spirits equally, and thus be the especial property of the whole only when united. Hunger for such possessions, as can be held by the pure soul, that you may accumulate

wealth for that united spirit of life which is your only true self. The peace you shall desire is that sacred peace which nothing can disturb, and in which the soul grows as does the holy flower upon the still lagoons. And that power which the disciple shall covet is that which shall make him appear as nothing in the eyes of men.

Desire possessions above all. But those possessions must belong to the pure spirit only, and be possessed therefore by all pure spirits equally, and thus be the especial property of the whole only when united.

It is God we must desire. Why, then, does the Master say "possessions"? Because everything that is has come out of God, and when we find God we find everything.

Someone asked Anandamayi Ma about what would remain once a person had transcended relativity, and they were told: "Nothing is lost there." So we leave everything behind, only to find it in the One. Here in relativity we cannot really possess anything because of the laws of change and dissolution. Moreover, instead of our possessing things, they begin to possess and bind us. But when we give them up, turn our back on them, and leave them behind, we will come to truly possess them in the possessing of God, for God wills to share all things with us and to say: "Thou art ever with me, and all that I have is thine" (Luke 15:31).

When we enter the Infinite, we will find everything there—we shall have gotten out of the mirror into the real thing. Right now we are living in the movie screen thinking that it is the real world. We have been afraid to move out into the light that is projected on the screen, thinking that we would become nothing. But if we keep on going further into the light, right to its very source, we will find that the whole "picture" is there, and has been all along.

To "desire possessions above all" is to desire Infinity: to desire to possess omnipotence, omniscience, and omnipresence. In transcending the universe we shall encompass it. But first we must get out of it.

Those who hold to it are the ones who lose it, but those who give it up come to possess it. Here in the realm of relativity we are grasping for mere reflections, trying to pull a reflection of the moon out of a lake by casting in a net.

The desired possessions are those things which belong only to the purified spirit when it returns to the Divine Source. All will possess them equally, for there God is all in all (I Corinthians 15:28). God shall be in us, not outside of us. We shall be with Him in the depths of our own being, just as we are even now in the depths of His being. And each of us shall possess the totality of God.

When Krishna was a child, those who loved him used to go out with him into the forests, and as he would play the flute they would dance around him. But one time each dancer found that Krishna was dancing with him. That is, there were as many Krishnas in the circle as there were dancers. So each one experienced dancing alone with Krishna. Each one had all of him. This is called the *Maharasa*, the Supreme Sweetness, each individual possessing all of God.

In possessing God we shall possess all that has ever been or ever will be. No need to wonder if we shall be bored! But only those who "give up" will gain. The "pure soul" means one that is clear and divested of all these bodies, "and thus be the especial property of the whole only when united." When we are one with God, then we will have it all.

We can—and should—desire this Divine Thing, this Divine Glory, this Divine All-possessiveness, this Divine Wealth, this Divine Kingdom. We are to hunger for it, but at the same time lose our hunger for all other things.

Hunger for such possessions, as can be held by the pure soul, that you may accumulate wealth for that united spirit of life which is your only true self.

By this is meant the Divine Wealth of spiritual perceptions in the highest levels of our being: not in that which is relative and time-space bound, but in that which is beyond it. In this way we shall be preparing ourselves for entry into the transcendent realms of existence, into the possession of the All.

The peace you shall desire is that sacred peace which nothing can disturb, and in which the soul grows as does the holy flower upon the still lagoons.

How much do we hear about peace in our modern times when there is less peace than ever before. And how violent are those who demand peace! The louder they yell the word, the less of the real thing there is. But it is not political peace the Master is speaking of, but "that sacred peace which nothing can disturb, and in which the soul grows as does the holy flower upon the still lagoons."

The holy flower referred to is the lotus, which in the East has for ages symbolized enlightenment and the enlightened soul. This lotus-peace is a sacred peace which nothing can disturb. Nothing can disturb it because it exists in that realm where "things" simply do not exist, where there is no "other" of any kind, but only unity. It exists in the core of our being where there is nothing else but God: which is why the Master says it is sacred.

The lotus grows "upon the still lagoons." All is at rest, yet down in the invisible depths the seed germinates and begins to grow. Down there all is mud and darkness, but the seed has a destiny for the light. It pushes up from the mud and begins the upward journey, growing in a spiral motion, in a form of cycles. Then it emerges onto the surface of the water in the full light of the sun where it blossoms in perfect beauty. The mud of its origin, and even its stalk, is ugly. Yet, from that ugliness proceeds beauty, a beauty that can manifest only outside of the water.

In silence in the depths of our being, the Divine Seed, the Holy Word, grows, lifting the consciousness higher and higher in evolution until the field of relativity ("water") is transcended and Divine Consciousness blossoms forth. This is clearly set forth in *Soham Yoga: The Yoga of the Self.*

And that power which the disciple shall covet is that which shall make him appear as nothing in the eyes of men.

Power that makes us appear as nothing! If it was earthly power, we would be considered great by men of earth, but the masters are not in their world, wielding earthly power, but live in the realm of God wielding the power of God. However great the miracles of the saints may be, they remain unknown to "the world," except to be mocked or denied by it. That is because the saints live in the spirit, and the world lives in the ego. Those in the ego consider the world of the spirit unreal, whereas those in the spirit know the ego and its world are unreal.

That power which enables us to be alone with God, even though in the world, makes us invisible to the world. Some of the greatest masters on earth have come in secret, lived in secret and departed in secret. This is true even now. There are people who are living next door to immortal masters and will never know it.

The power we should covet is that which will make us appear as nothing in the eyes of men. Why? Because the outer eyes of men only see matter, and their inner eyes see only ego. If, then, there is nothing in us of earth and ego, how will they see us? This is why earthbound people meet teachers of only middling evolution, who still have plenty of ego and ignorance, and are deeply impressed with them and even adore them. Then they will meet a truly evolved person and not give him a second thought, except maybe to remark to someone how unimpressed they were. The lives of saints are filled with accounts of people who came to meet them and then refused to believe they were the saints they had heard so much about. Often they actually despise them.

Pilgrims used to make long journeys to Zagorsk to meet Saint Sergius of Radonezh. They would ask one of the monks where the abbot (Saint Sergius) was, and when he was pointed out to them, they would become angry and say: "Quit trying to make a fool of me. That old man cannot be the abbot! Now which one is he, really?"

In Egypt a translator for the Coptic Patriarchate told me that once a large group of Protestant theological students came from Germany to see Pope Shenouda. The Pope came in wearing his simple monastic clothes as usual and spoke to them, answering questions, for over an hour. Then he excused himself and left. The group then asked the translator: "When do we meet the Pope?" The translator told them they had just been speaking to him. They objected, saying: "That old man was nice, but he could not be the Pope." When the translator and others assured them that they had truly met the Pope, they became angry and began to shout: "Don't you think we are good enough to meet your Pope? Do you think we are so stupid that you can pass that old man off on us as the Pope?" Only when some of the bishops came and solemnly swore to them that "that old man" really was the Pope would they accept it. Having met Pope Shenouda and spoken with him at length quite a few times, I can assure you that he was in no way "just an old man," but those without eyes cannot see.

People used to come to see Sri Ramakrishna, and assume from his simple demeanor and dress that he was a servant. They would call out: "Hey, you, tell me where the Paramhansa lives!" He would say: "Here in this room." In they would go, and he would come in another door and sit down. How amazed they would be. On occasion such people even made him carry things they had brought to present to "the saint."

On occasion, though, evil people hate the saints on sight, which is why the master tells us to desire the power that will make us seem like nothing to them. Then they will leave us alone. We can only gauge the spiritual status of others from our own status. Those who are wandering in the maze of earthly delusion cannot in any way sense or comprehend those who are out of the game and home free. Who but God is egoless enough to be as nothing in the eyes of the ignorant, yet love and bless them? So are His saints, who are His perfect images.

In this world we are strangers and pilgrims. Therefore we must live like strangers and pilgrims, estranging ourselves from this world by snapping the bonds which we have ignorantly formed with it. Does not the world utterly disregard God? How many in the world strut around, saying: "We don't see the need for God to exist," "God has been created by man," "Man creates God in his own image," and suchlike platitudes. But God continues to love and believe in them. This is the anonymity we must desire.

17. Seek out the way.

Seek out the way: for there *is* a way. One of the basic misconceptions that many Westerners have about reincarnation is the idea that we need do nothing specific to accomplish our personal evolution, that we need only be born over and over again, learning from each life and thereby becoming increasingly intelligent and creative. And in the meantime we can have everything we want, either in one life or in another. In other words, rebirth is seen as a gigantic cycle of evolutionary self-indulgence.

The truth is, through our ignorance and misapplication of our divine powers we have turned this world into a prison and each birth into a sentence of imprisonment. Of course, just as in civil prisons very wealthy people often furnish their cells with every luxury and live there in complete comfort and self-indulgence, so many of us manage to have lives in which we have wealth and advantages. But that cannot change the fundamental truth that we are in bondage or the fact that in the next birth our life may be as miserable and deprived as this one was satisfying and fulfilled.

Therefore we must get away from the compulsion of birth and death, and for that we need a way of escape. There must be an actual path, a practical system of extrication from ignorance. The Master is speaking of such a way, not just theory. Various disciplines and practices comprise this way. But it is not readily at hand, at least not to our perceptions, so we must seek it out.

Seeking out the way is a characteristic of spiritual awakening. Those who are awake seek, and those who still sleep do not. It is just that simple. There are many seekers, but only those are finders who seek the way out through spiritual rebirth and self-evolution that result in transcendence of birth and death. They are the seekers of whom the Master is speaking. He is not even giving a thought to those who seek lesser things.

When we look at the world around us, we see people floundering in ignorance, destroying themselves literally, because they are not seeking God. Seeing this, we often conceive the delusive idea that we must awaken them and point them toward God. But it cannot be done. Spiritual consciousness cannot be awakened by an external force. We can awaken someone from physical unconsciousness, and even from intellectual ignorance through education. But spiritual awakening comes only from the Divine Spirit working from within the individual spirit.

Buddha usually stayed in forests and isolated areas, having nothing to do with so-called civilization. Once a disciple reproached him for not going to where people were to help alleviate their suffering. In response, Buddha sent him to a large city to ask each person there what he would wish for if he could have anything he desired. It took him a long time, but at last he accomplished his mission and returned to Buddha. When Buddha asked him how his mission had gone, the disciple replied with disgust that every person had only wanted foolish or petty things. "How many wanted enlightenment?" asked Buddha. "None," came the answer. "Then why do you want me to force on them what they do not even want?" demanded Buddha. And the disciple got the idea.

The soul must awaken itself. We must not try to arouse spiritual consciousness (which is also love of God) in another person, for it must arise of itself. It is certainly right to work on stirring up our own spiritual consciousness, though, for if we were not already awake to some degree we would not desire to do so or even know that it is possible. Just as we cannot force the fruit to form and ripen on the tree, so we must not attempt such a folly with the souls of others. We do not burden children with the concerns of adulthood, and in the same way we need to leave spiritual infants undisturbed. Just as we let children prattle on in nonsense, so we should not challenge any foolishness the spiritual infants express, but just patiently listen. All we will accomplish by attempting to awaken them and get them to adopt our way of seeing things will be to arouse them to resentment and ego-defensive argument.

Each of us must seek out the way himself.

18. Seek the way by retreating within.

The Master previously said we are to *seek out* the way. Lest we misunderstand and think that our seeking should be external, he continues: "Seek the way by retreating within." Carl Jung said: "Who looks outside, dreams. Who looks inside, awakens." We must withdraw our consciousness from the outer illusions of "things" and focus it on interior realities. The Master is not speaking of meditation now, but of simply gathering up our scattered forces and becoming self-contained.

So the first step is to gather ourselves up into ourselves. We must pull ourselves together and learn to be still. We must make ourselves coherent again. Having been spread out like a puddle on the floor, we must now come back to a semblance of shape. To do this we must gather in our forces, not expending our energies on anything external: not only through the senses, but through the mind, as well.

The retreat within is likened by the yogis of India to the drawing in of its head and legs by a tortoise. The wise learn to pull all the extensions of themselves back into their source and become whole again. When this is done, and we are restored to our original integrity, then a real beginning of conscious evolution is possible. Meditation is the process to accomplish this.

This divine retreat is treated very systematically by the Indian sage, Patanjali, in his *Yoga Sutras*. (See the book *Yoga: Science of the Absolute*.) There he outlines the eight steps to unitive consciousness. They are: Yama-Niyama, Asana, Pranayama, Pratyahara, Dharana, Dhyana, and Samadhi.

Yama-Niyama consists of that which ought to be done (yama), and that which should not be done (niyama). In other words, the avoidance of vice and the cultivation of virtue. This is the fundamental step because this changes the vibration of our entire energy complex, from the gross to the most subtle bodies–which include the mind, intellect, and will. It also cuts off the production of negative karmas and begins the production of positive karmas which will expedite our eventual transcendence of all karmas.

Asana is the posture for meditation, which need not be the difficult Lotus Posture, but any upright position that is easy and steady. This also means the positioning of the mind in a state of relaxation and ease.

Pranayama is control of the life forces–not breathing exercises, as is commonly supposed. Fundamentally pranayama means the refining (making subtle) of the breath, and its lengthening through spontaneous slowing down of the respiratory rate. As the Master has said, we must "seek the way by retreating within." That is, we need to draw our energies back within ourselves. Presently we are a field of dispersed energies. We need to draw them back in toward their centers and become a more compact field of energy. This is accomplished by–and is–pranayama.

Pratyahara is the interiorization of the mind, the becoming aware of interior consciousness and getting the mind acclimatized to interior states and processes.

Dharana is the fixing of the mind (attention) on a particular point, object, or thought.

Dhyana is meditation, which Patanjali defines as the continuous flow of the mind toward God, like an uninterrupted stream of oil.

The final step is *samadhi*, which is the experience of union with God in which we must become permanently established.

Dharana, dhyana, and samadhi are the process of going within. We boldly go inside and start looking around. At the same time we are to be detached: indifferent to anything that happens or that we perceive. We have to remain in a state of balance, extremely aware without being caught by any interior experiences. We are to be intensely aware without getting involved and losing ourselves in that involvement. It is a paradox, but we are to both ignore and perceive them. That is why we neither accept nor reject what arises in the sphere of our awareness. We are boldly indifferent! And through that detached attitude we affect our interior status in ways that would be impossible if we were reacting to what arises.

Here again is another example of how in esoteric practice and life we must learn to go in two directions at once. This takes courage on occasion, and that is why the Master tells us to be bold, as was Jesus when He remained silent, refusing to reply to Pilate's interrogations (John 19:9). Jumping into the water and letting ourselves sink takes a lot of nerve, and so does leaping into the mind and letting whatever comes, come. Courageous objectivity is needed.

We must never fall into the pitfall of classifying our meditations into "good meditations" and "bad meditations." All meditations are good when done correctly. Definitely, the experiences in meditation can be pleasant, unpleasant, or tedious, but that has no bearing on the quality of the meditation itself. Here, too, we must be dispassionate, accepting whatever comes. Perhaps the boring and seemingly futile and empty times of meditation take the most nerve to endure. But they are usually the most productive when viewed in retrospect.

Going boldly within is not like the stereotypic great white hunter, plunging into the mental jungle with gun pointed and knife between the teeth. It is just the opposite.

19. Seek the way by advancing boldly without.

Since "retreating" sounds passive and carries connotations of having been routed in battle, the Master gives us the second phase of the process so we will understand that our retreat is part of a dynamic, not a passive, process: "Seek the way by advancing boldly without." That is, having gone within and having our intuitive sense awakened, we can now move in the outer world with an illumined vision, understanding the nature of what we encounter, and be able to use it for our progress. Outside of meditation we objectify what has taken place during our retreat within. And our inner experience has made us stronger and able to cope with the outer world.

Those who become "sensitive" and unable to endure contact with the world about them, always seeking to "retreat" from it, are not practicing right meditation, or are doing it incorrectly. I know a man who has for years been involved with one of the large guru/yoga cults. Wherever he goes out visiting with his wife he carries with him a little wood "bench." The moment he enters he finds a place off to the side, puts it down and sits on it, kneeling and sitting as is done in many oriental countries (not India). Then he sits bolt upright, closes his eyes and begins to "meditate," though his facial expressions show response to whatever he hears going on around him. When the visit is over, he picks up the little bench and leaves. A woman who sponsors a group in the same cult will go to a social gathering and sit there in silence, occasionally smiling in a sickly manner. After about half and hour she inquires as to where a "quiet" place is so she can "meditate." Then she goes there for quite some time, then re-enters with glowing eyes and a fatuous smile. (After all, God is bliss.) She usually leaves before anyone else does, saying nothing but making a big show of her silent departure. Neither of these two cultists can cope with any form of real life.

20. Seek it not by any one road. To each temperament there is one road which seems the most desirable. But the way is not found by devotion alone, by religious contemplation alone, by ardent progress, by self-sacrificing labor, by studious observation of life. None alone can take the disciple more than one step onward. All steps are necessary to make up the ladder. The vices of men become steps in the ladder, one by one, as they are surmounted. The virtues of man are steps indeed, necessary—not by any means to be dispensed with. Yet, though they create a fair atmosphere and a happy future, they are useless if they stand alone. The whole nature of man must be used wisely by the one who desires to enter the way. Each man is to himself absolutely the way, the truth, and the life. But he is only so when he grasps his whole individuality firmly, and, by the force of his awakened spiritual will, recognizes this individuality as not himself, but that thing which he has with pain created for his own use, and by means of which he purposes, as his growth slowly develops his intelligence, to reach to the life beyond individuality. When he knows that for this his wonderful complex separated life exists, then, indeed, and then only, he is upon the way. Seek it by plunging into the mysterious and glorious depths of your own inmost being. Seek it by testing all experience, by utilizing the senses in order to understand the growth and meaning of individuality, and the beauty and obscurity of those other divine fragments which are struggling side by side with you, and form the race to which you belong. Seek it by study of the laws of being, the laws of nature, the laws of the supernatural: and seek it by making the profound obeisance of the soul to the dim star that burns within. Steadily, as you watch and worship, its light will grow stronger. Then you may know you have found the

beginning of the way. And when you have found the end its light will suddenly become the infinite light.

Seek it not by any one road.

That is, we must take care of all angles and aspects of our being and consciousness, neglecting nothing. Some people think that meditation can be used as a gimmick for enlightenment without there being any need to provide the right conditions for its effectiveness. We can think of it like agriculture. Plowing is not everything in itself, nor is watering, or sowing, or fertilizing, or planting. But they must all go together if we are to reap a harvest for our efforts. If one thing is left out then failure is inevitable. Both our interior and exterior lives must be ordered and maintained according to the laws of spiritual evolution. This is what yama and niyama are all about.

To each temperament there is one road which seems the most desirable.

The adjective "desirable" shows that the Master is speaking of the egoic reaction that if it feels, tastes or appears good, then it *is* good: which of course has nothing at all to do with whether a thing really is or is not good. The ego always mistakes the pleasant and the pleasing for the good: which never is either pleasant nor pleasing to the ego, though the spirit rejoices in it.

This is how the Katha Upanishad explains it: "The good is one thing; the pleasant is another. These two, differing in their ends, both prompt to action. Blessed are they that choose the good; they that choose the pleasant miss the goal. Both the good and the pleasant present themselves to men. The wise, having examined both, distinguish the one from the other. The wise prefer the good to the pleasant; the foolish, driven by fleshly desires, prefer the pleasant to the good. (Katha Upanishad 1:2:1-2)

What are the "roads" the Master has in mind? He will now enumerate them.

But the way is not found by devotion alone, by religious contemplation alone, by ardent progress, by self-sacrificing labor, by studious observation of life. None alone can take the disciple more than one step onward. All steps are necessary to make up the ladder.

This being so, we need to make this statement a mental checklist, especially when we feel we are not progressing as we should, to help us determine if we are really doing all we need to do. It would be good to take each one in turn and look at it well.

By devotion the Master does not mean the sentimental, emotional type of devotion, but rather dedication: intense devotion to the search for enlightenment. It also implies devoting the entire life to the search, and not just a bit of life that can be conveniently eked out of an otherwise full agenda. The search for God must be the heart of the seeker's entire life. In fact, it must embrace the whole of the seeker's life so that whatever the activity engaged in, it is seen as part of the search.

Steadiness is also indicated here, for spiritual life must be continuous, not a series of startings and stoppings. Momentum is a key factor in spiritual success. Continual practice is the means to accomplish this. Sacrifice is also implied here, but that will be spoken of shortly.

Meditation is essential. But the egos of mankind have invented many false processes and methods that are devoid of spiritual content to suit those to whom communion with God is distasteful and therefore undesirable. It is not to those that the Master is speaking, and to ensure this is understood, he has specified *religious* contemplation as one of the ways, not just contemplation.

This also has a twofold implication. The first is that the practice of meditation is a God-centered religious practice. The second is that true meditation is a spiritual activity, not intellectual or emotional. It is an action of the ever-free spirit, not of mind, intellect, or emotion (feeling). For this reason meditation cannot involve these lesser aspects of our makeup. So all linkages to them, such as discursive prayers, visualizations, imaginations, concepts or intellectual ponderings, or self-induced (imagined) feelings of peace, love, etc., must have no place in our meditation. God being beyond form or conceptualization, even beyond the idea that He *is*, our meditations must be beyond all such as well. As the sages of both East and West have said, we must enter into the Divine Darkness, into the Cloud of Unknowing, where we shall both see and know as we are seen and known.

By employing the term "ardent progress" the Master implies intensity, urgency, and singleness of purpose: to be afire for God. This is no shallow spiritual weekending, but a race unto the Ultimate Goal. God is a consuming fire (Deuteronomy 4:24; 9:3; Hebrews 12:29), and all that is not divine is dissolved by entering into his Being. As Sri Ramakrishna often said: "A salt doll once went to measure the depth of the ocean. But when it entered the ocean it was melted. Who, then, was to return to report the ocean's depth?"

Before leaving this subject we should distinguish between the ardent progress the Master holds forth and mere rapid change which usually has no depth or lasting effect. The latter is like that of the hare in the story of the tortoise and the hare. There can be no perseverance in spiritual life without the developing of interior consciousness, which is also spiritual evolution, and that can only be produced through meditation. Those who rush around to lectures and seminars, devouring books and articles by the pound, babbling on and on in rhapsody about finding the truth at last and how their spiritual horizons are widening (but not deepening: that is the rub), are like firework rockets, quickly burning themselves out in a spectacular ascent only to fall back to earth to sink deeper into ignorance than they were before.

Those who quietly apply themselves in patience and perseverance like the tortoise are the ones who win through to the heavenly vision.

Spiritual genius, like any other genius, is also one percent inspiration and ninety-nine percent perspiration. Therefore much work comes before any hope of glory. Yet, labor is not enough. It must be self-sacrificing, according to the Master. Why is this? Obviously because labor in the spirit is a means of cutting off (sacrificing) our identity with the lesser, material and psychic sides of our being. Also, sacrifice is a statement of value. Nothing ventured, nothing gained; nothing spent, nothing bought. "You get what you pay for" and "There is no such thing as a free lunch" may sound mundane and even a touch vulgar, but they are nonetheless as true in the spirit as they are in the world. Therefore, correct spiritual labor both frees us from lower identity and wins for us a niche in the higher realms.

Sacrifice is a statement of value, as has been said, and the effort of sacrifice keeps reminding us of our ideals. During the persecutions of Catholics in England, one priest was kept in the attic of a jail, chained by his legs. The shackles caused terrible sores to develop on his legs, so his friends paid the jailer to take them off. When next they came to visit the priest they found the chains back on as before. "I paid him even more money to put them on me again," he explained, "for every time I move my legs the clinking of the chains reminds me to Whom I belong." Love does such things.

Not idle observation of life, but studious observation is necessary to form a correct evaluation of life and its elements. Even more, studious observation can reveal the very nature of life itself. In this case, since it is relative existence that is meant by "life," studious observation will reveal it to be no life at all but a state of death which must be passed beyond if we would live. But first we have to see it, in the sense of full comprehension. "Have you not seen what life is?" was a question asked by Anandamayi Ma.

A woman whose husband was continually beating her always made excuses for him, refusing to see his real nature. After some years, one day he lifted a club to strike and perhaps kill her. Suddenly she cried out: "Now I see you for what you are!" Dropping the club, her husband ran away, never to be seen again. In the same way, all that we are ignorantly wedded to will vanish in a moment once we see it truly. Only God remains when finally seen as he is.

"Studious" also implies objectivity. That is, when we do finally see through life, it will cause no pain, but rather bring peace. We will not complain about the emptiness of worldly life, but will happily abide in the real life which will then have dawned in our consciousness.

The vices of men become steps in the ladder, one by one, as they are surmounted.

This is important to keep in mind so that whenever we encounter a problem within our mind we need not despair or condemn ourselves, but simply apply ourselves to changing it from a pitfall into a rung on the ladder of our progress. Every behavioral and mental pattern is a kind of vortex spinning in the energy field of the mind. They are what we might call "energy mechanisms" in our aura, configurations of energy that produce mental and physical states. When spinning (polarized) one way, they draw us downward; but when repolarized (reversed) they lift us up just as surely and efficiently. Therefore every element in our life can be transmuted into a force for our perfection. This is why great sinners can become great saints. When we see a person seemingly full of vice, we are seeing a person potentially full of virtue.

Everything being dual, every vice is the underside of a virtue. For example, cowardice is prudence gone wrong, and hostility is courage gone wrong. So we transmute the vice into virtue, for the virtue is already there, the vice only being its distortion. This is the sense in which evil does not exist, but really is an aberration of good. We do not accept and indulge the negative pattern, but get busy and reform it, turning it back to its original, correct status. And that is true "repentance" in the Biblical sense which means a total turnaround in thought, word and deed.

Since the presence of vice is the presence of virtue, we need not be discouraged but take hope, for goodness is at hand. There are some motor-driven wheels that will spin according to the direction they are moved at the onset. To get them to move in the opposite way they need only be stopped and then set going again in the other direction. Electrical motors themselves will go in the opposite direction if we simply switch the wiring of the poles. (A friend of mine bought a juicer in a thrift store, and when he turned it on it was going in the wrong direction. But when he got its wiring reversed then he got juice.) Changing our mental operations is just as simple and as precise. It may not always be easy, but it is always possible and inevitable. Patience, optimism and right effort are all that is needed.

So the Master is telling us that we need not worry about vice as such, but instead to use the tools he has just enumerated to transform it into virtue and lift ourselves by its transmutation. For the practices he has named do change us. As we surmount the vices one by one, we rise into higher and higher reaches of consciousness.

The virtues of man are steps indeed, necessary—not by any means to be dispensed with.

The Master is aware that some people misunderstand when they hear that they need not bewail their vices, and so they begin to accommodate and indulge them. But such things must not be allowed to continue as vices but be turned into virtues, virtues which the Master assures us cannot be laid aside for a moment, for they are absolutely necessary. Without them there is no spiritual progress, for the virtues are the tools by which we cultivate spiritual consciousness.

Yet, though they create a fair atmosphere and a happy future, they are useless if they stand alone.

These virtues produce a positive vibration in our life and create good karma, but they are useless if they stand alone. Instead they must be applied to something: that is, they must be *used*. They are not just to be cultivated like flowers for the viewing, so people will say how nice and good we are. If they are not used as tools in the search for God, they are then as nothing. There are virtuous people who are not seeking God, and in them the virtues are spiritually meaningless.

The whole nature of man must be used wisely by the one who desires to enter the way.

The first step in spiritual life, then, is to gain mastery of every aspect of our nature. By "nature" the Master means that which in Sanskrit is called *prakriti*, the entire range of energies which go to make up what we call a human being. We must use these energies to get beyond them into the realms of higher evolution and ultimately into pure spirit.

In the Bhagavad Gita we find these words: "One acts according to one's own prakriti–even the wise man does so. Beings follow their own prakriti; what will restraint accomplish?" (3:33). It is not uncommon that a person of negative behavior suddenly sees the folly of his ways and for a while becomes exemplary. And then one day everything goes back to the way it was before, or even worse. Why? Because he changed his behavior by the power of his will, but he never changed the negative vibration of his subtle life energies, his prakriti. He controlled and repressed it, but did not change it. So eventually it all came to nothing.

Just as we must go through the vices, making them into steps of virtue, so must we use all of the aspects of our nature, even though they are just vibrating energies and not our true Self. We must use them to seek the Self. By yoga gradually the aspirant gains perfect control of all the bodies and the energies of which they are composed and orients

85

them toward higher consciousness, establishing in them the control of the highest centers of awareness and power.

We gain control of our whole nature so we can use it in the transmutation of consciousness that alone is the search for God. Strictly speaking, the term "search for God" can be misleading. Since God is not only everywhere, but is the root essence of our very being, where would we "go" to "find" Him? He is not only "here," it is he alone who makes up all that is the "here" and "there" of our experience. As one great Sufi saint wrote: "I laugh to hear of fish athirst in the water." We do not need to find God, we need to *know* God—and *be* God.

How well I remember my childhood frustration when I could not read music. All I needed was to understand those markings on the page, and wonder of wonders! I would be able to make music. Even more, I remember the first time I could comprehend those markings and translate them into music. The tune was simple and eminently forgettable, but it was music, and I was on my way.

Jung was asked in an interview: "Do you believe there is a God?" "No!" was his immediate and emphatic response, "I do not *believe* there is a God, I *know* there is a God." Presently the energies in which we (our spirit-consciousness) are encased blind us to reality. But the same energies repolarized illumine the way to Knowing. Though they cannot reveal the reality, they are necessary to reveal the path inward to divine vision, in which seeing and knowing are one and the same.

As long as we are in the realm of relativity we must act. Even the quest for enlightenment is an action. Thus we need all the energies possible for utilization in our journey to God. Without yoga sadhana this is impossible. There are energy reservoirs in the body which influence (and usually control) our behavior. By means of yogic practices these energies must be put to their intended use in our evolutionary unfoldment. Even negative energies can be used by turning them back to their original positive condition. When we both can and do master them, we shall be on our way to ourselves becoming masters.

Each man is to himself absolutely the way, the truth, and the life.

We have nothing to work with but ourselves, no other reality to be involved with but ourselves. There is the Supreme Reality, God, Who is also our reality, but we have lost touch with our consciousness of that truth and are immersed in the illusion of independent existence which also cuts us off from true knowledge of our individual self-reality. This being so, the first step to God is knowledge and mastery of ourselves. Then we can proceed deeper to the root-being of ourselves: God. Self-realization comes before God-realization.

There is no power for us to work with except that which we already have. We must release that power from within, not get it from anything "outside," including God. We have already been given everything we need. We are *kata holos*: we contain everything. God has given us everything we need, both within and without, so that when we do turn to God and seek for Him we will succeed.

One of the indications that egoic "love" is not worthy love at all is the cliche "I need you," which really means: "I can use you for my own satisfaction." This may be flattering to human egos, but God wants nothing of it. Therefore he has ensured that we can stay out in the realm of relativity, playing with the infinite variety of illusions forever, if we are so inclined. Only when real love awakens can we retrace our steps to the Divine Source.

God has made us of "independent means" so we will seek Him for Himself alone. In that search we ourselves are the way, in the sense that we do not look to an external path to find God, but turn within and return within to our source: God. So we are ourselves the path we must tread back home. We are the truth in the sense that it is our own reality we must come to know, for when we come to the root of our reality or being we will find God, the Reality of our reality. We are the life in the same sense for God is the Life of our life.

There is a story in the Far East of a man who was imprisoned in the top room of a tower. To rescue him, his wife tied a silk thread to the back leg of a large beetle. Then she put a drop of honey on the horns of the beetle and put the beetle on the wall of the tower, aimed straight up. Wanting the honey, the beetle kept crawling forward, right up the tower. When it reached the top, the man caught hold of the silk thread. His wife then tied a cotton string onto its end. He pulled up the silk thread and got the string. She then tied a heavy cord to the string. After that she tied a small rope onto the cord, and he pulled that up. Last, she tied a heavy rope on the end of the small rope. When he had pulled that up to the top, he tied it around a stone post, climbed down it, and escaped. So it is in spiritual life. From mastery of the lesser we can proceed to mastery of the greater. First we master our physical makeup, then our mental, and then our spiritual. From conquest of our spirit we can rise to possess the Kingdom of God: the Consciousness of Infinite Spirit.

But he is only so when he grasps his whole individuality firmly, and, by the force of his awakened spiritual will, recognizes this individuality as not himself, but that thing which he has with pain created for his own use, and by means of which he purposes, as his growth slowly develops his intelligence, to reach to the life beyond individuality.

"But he is only so when he grasps his whole individuality firmly." Partial control is not sufficient; we must master the entirety of our being. This is both so there will be no imbalance in the process of transmutation and also because we are seeking to defragment ourselves and return to our original state of unity. Therefore all the "passengers" must be "on board" before the journey can be begun, much less completed.

There is another aspect of this. Spiritual egotism is always a threat to the seeker, and one of its favorite tricks is to make us unduly elated over a single step in our progress, hoping to blind us to the necessity of taking many more steps before we can be "home safe." It would like us to stop along the way and become so engrossed in self-congratulation that we think we have attained all there is to attain.

An aunt of mine was determined that her little son be a prodigy at the keyboard. She would take him from one piano teacher to another. Each in turn would suggest that he wait until he was more mature, and would salve her ego by saying: "But your son has a beautiful 'touch.'" She would relay this ebulliently to everyone. So it became a joke in our family when one of us had failed at something, to say: "But I have a beautiful 'touch'!" Small comfort.

The Master wants us to know that to fail in one point is to fail in all. "For whoever shall keep the whole law, and yet stumble in one point, he is guilty of all" (James 2:10). That may sound unduly severe, but it is not a judgment, it is a fact of spiritual life.

Why does the Master speak of individuality? Are we not to transcend that? Yes, but we must distinguish between the individuality of the ego and the individuality of the spirit. The egoic individuality consists of personality traits, conditionings, and karmas. The individuality of the spirit is its innate divinity.

The lesser parts of our being are the mirrors in which the divine individuality is to be reflected and radiated outward to the healing of our environment as well as us. The ego has wrested them away from the control of our spirit and turned them to reflect its false face. Erroneous philosophies therefore counsel us to smash the mirrors to become free and perfect. The correct thing is to repossess those mirrors and turn them back to their original orientation, and to behold in them our true face of spirit which in turn will mirror back the face of God, for the individual spirit is His reflection just as our various bodies are meant to mirror us. When this is done, the process of divine transmutation or deification (theosis) is complete.

Just as we sometimes only master a part of our individual makeup and want to believe we have mastered all, so we sometimes are satisfied with only a tenuous grasp. This is why the Master says "grasps firmly" in his exposition. We must be established in that control. Often someone gets just a glimpse of his destined glory and mistakenly assumes that he has attained that glory and vanquished the enemy. Then the ego reasserts itself and casts him down from his imagined height, hoping to thus demoralize him and cause him to give up his efforts in disgust and disillusionment. If the ego cannot destroy us through pride, then it will try to paralyze us through shame and guilt. For this reason the Master warns us to be strong in our grip.

Where does illumination come from? Some schools say it comes from God like a strike of lightning. Some say it comes automatically from evolution, without need of thought or aspiration. But the Master speaks of this requisite insight as coming "by the force of his awakened spiritual will." None of us doubt that some force is needed, or that it is the force of will that is the needed power, but the two words "awakened" and "spiritual" complete the picture for us. Nowadays there is a lot of talk about kundalini, and most of its modern exponents treat the awakening of kundalini as a kind of psychedelic volcanic eruption and fireworks display. The truth is, the awakening of kundalini is the awakening of the spiritual will. If the bodies of the aspirant have been balanced, purified, and refined as they should, then no cataclysmic displays occur. The individual will definitely be aware of the awakening and the resulting change, but it will be perfectly internalized with no external manifestations at all. Also, it will be far more dramatic than the gross phenomena incorrectly considered its corollaries.

The will that must be awakened is that of the spirit. There are other, lesser wills (really addictions and compulsions) that have gripped and bound us throughout the ages. As the ego is the false self, so they are false wills. But that in no way diminishes their destructive effect on us.

The lesser, delusive wills are dissolved at the awakening and coming into mastery of the divine will of the divine Self.

We all believe that we have free will, but do we? Desires and aspirations we have in abundance, as well as many compulsions, but none of them are exercises of will, rather they are manifestations of lack of will, of our being shaped and impelled by forces other than ourselves. Conditionings galore and behavioral programmings innumerable are ours, but all from outside us, imposed upon us. Nothing of will, free or otherwise, is among them. Like railway trains, we run on the tracks others have laid down for us. We show little imagination in our life. No one ever thinks of doing anything unusual. Everybody is just going to get the job, the wife or husband, the children, the car and the house: all usually mediocre. Who ever thinks of finding God, much less dedicating their entire life to the search for God?

The will has to be awakened, and then the real labor begins for us as we begin learning to exercise the spiritual will. It must be under our complete control. This is why the aspirant must prepare himself by disciplines which strengthen the will. We can be to ourselves "the way, the truth and the life" only when we have grasped our whole individuality "by the force of awakened spiritual will." But that awakened will is to go further than mere control. By the power of that spiritual will the struggler then "recognizes this individuality as not himself."

Those who think that their bodies, emotions, minds, intellects, etc., are truly themselves, through that very identification become enslaved to those things. They think they are using them when in reality they are being dragged along by them. Immoral people, for example, who spend their whole days and nights thinking of just how to exploit their senses (especially the sense of sex) think they are masters, when in reality they are slaves. Because they are living in the mirror everything is seen backwards.

Now we come to a statement of great import. When a man has grasped his whole individuality firmly, then he, "by the force of his awakened spiritual will, recognizes this individuality as not himself." A little reflection reveals how this will be so. The eye cannot see itself, the hand cannot grasp itself, the foot cannot kick itself: all those actions can only be done in relation to external objects. This being so, when we grasp hold of and master the various levels of our being we will perceive them as external to ourselves and not ourselves at all. This is why the spiritual will is required to accomplish this. For the lesser wills cannot be turned to the mastery of themselves.

Actually, to even begin the mastery of these lower entities through our spiritual will we must first be posited in our spiritual nature, which is itself spiritual *consciousness*. The only way to be a master is to not be in any way identified with what is mastered. If we listen to the whines and complaints of the not-self and sympathize with it and indulge it, we will never be its master. We must be completely objective toward it.

What is the individuality of the aspirant? It is "that thing which he has with pain created for his own use." Indeed, have we not suffered to get to this point? A brief look at nature reveals the constant struggle, suffering, danger and death in which all sentient beings live. Even the bugs that bite us have bugs that bite them! How painful and exhaustive is the climb up to animal form, and infinitely more so the ascent from animal to human. And all of that has been our own doing, our own creation.

Only with great pain have we come to this level of evolution, so is it not tragic that we would waste it in doing something else besides attaining spiritual liberation? Or after all the agony of billions of lives, to then use our status only to simply run a successful business, for example? Think of taking creation cycles to get to this human body, and then to expend (and perhaps destroy) it in the pursuit of temporary material pleasure or gain. What ridiculous things we do with this fantastic instrument that we have created. It is like using FM radio for trashy music, or taking a great work of art and using it for a doorstop.

More than once in recorded history barbarians have used works of art and books of fine literature for fuel.

It is spiritually insane for a human being not to utilize his life in the search for God, and his self-degradation produces great sufferings as a consequence. The subverting of our divinity can only result in infinite misery.

Once at a spiritual conference (Samyam Sapta) I heard Anandamayi Ma tell of having seen a divine being in the form of a young boy who sang over and over: "Having acquired a human body, call on God. And having filled your mind with God, then go to the world of God." In other words, we have become humans so we can become gods. It is absurd that anyone would use the excuse: "I am not ready yet. I am not evolved enough. I have this to do and I have that to do first. Then maybe I will be ready." The moment we enter the human form we are ready for Self- and God-realization.

"He... recognizes this individuality as not himself, but that thing which he has with pain created for his own use." It is not a trap, a prison, as we have let it become, but it is an instrument for our freedom. Nothing could be more fallacious than to attempt to drop or dissolve it in the hope of that way attaining enlightenment. Modern distortions of Eastern philosophies may say so, but the true masters teach just the opposite. For it is that "by means of which he purposes, as his growth slowly develops his intelligence, to reach to the life beyond individuality."

We have only one purpose: to go beyond this relative existence. Why did we even come here, then? For that very transcendence. Does it seem absurd? It should not, for do we not enroll in school for the very purpose of one day graduating from it and leaving it behind forever? By this "creation" of our individuality which is in relativity, and which is the means of integrating us with relativity, we can go beyond relativity. It has no other purpose. To engage it in any other pursuit is to be something less than human.

What is evolution? There are many definitions, but the master describes its nature by describing its effect when he says that the individual's "growth slowly develops his intelligence." Please note that he says intelligence, not intellect. Intellect, like the mind, is only an instrument of intelligence. Intelligence is the scope of our consciousness. The greater our field of consciousness, the greater is our intelligence, something academicians miss completely through their involvement with intellect. To be intelligent is to be conscious. There are no pen and pencil tests to measure true intelligence, it is lived out in the individual's passage to the Infinite.

The Master knows, then, that the expansion of consciousness is a slow though steady growth. Spiritual life is neither an instant turn-on nor a one-step jump to the Infinite. It is a gradual process that occurs in precise steps and stages. Moreover, it has but one purpose: to go beyond its confines into the Infinite Consciousness.

When he knows that for this his wonderful complex separated life exists, then, indeed, and then only, he is upon the way.

The separated life is meant for the united life. We have come out from God so we could go back to God in "a more perfect union," as it says in the Preamble to the Constitution of the United States.

"When he knows... he is on the way," affirms the Master. This cannot be a matter of mere belief because others have told us or because it appears reasonable and acceptable to the intellect. We must *know* that our destiny lies in God. We must have looked at ourselves and understood our nature. And we must have looked at the unself and understood its nature, too.

Many are those who say: "I have been on the Path for years," just because they belong to some metaphysical organization(s), have read metaphysical books, and can reel off the requisite cliches. This is not really being "on the way." Being on the way is the active engaging of all our power to tread the way constantly, not just a little bit. Nor is it the complacent attitude: "I will just be born over and over again, and evolve from life to life." The person who is on the way is one who is actively working on his self-evolution.

Seek it by plunging into the mysterious and glorious depths of your own inmost being.

This is the way: the way within. Before we get to those glorious depths of the inmost consciousness, however, we have to descend through a lot that is not glorious. For this reason meditation can sometimes be exceedingly tedious, even unpleasant, uncomfortable and upsetting as we pass from level to level of our upper and middle layers. But this kind of psychic inventory-taking is quite necessary. The meditation process is showing us all the aspects of our being. This is because it is bringing us into mastery of them, and for that full awareness of them is needed.

A great deal of meditation that we may mistakenly think of as wasted because we are not seeing lights or visions or levitating, is really this taking of inventory. We are usually out of touch with all these aspects, but if we do not pass all the soldiers in review, how will we become commander of the army? "My mind wanders so much in meditation," we say, and sometimes it is true. But we must be sure we are not mistaking this inventory-taking for mental wandering–and that we do not mistake mental wandering for inventory-taking. We must not get caught up or distracted by those perceptions, but at the same time we must never turn away from what is being shown us, for that will prevent our correction of what we are viewing.

Before we are ready for the pure awareness of God, we must first become aware of our inner workings. So we seek the way by "plunging into the mysterious and glorious depths of" our "own inmost being."

Seek it by testing all experience, by utilizing the senses in order to under-stand the growth and meaning of individuality,...

The senses referred to here are predominately the interior senses, astral and causal. Even when we look at something with the external eyes we can bring the inner sight into play, as well. Sometimes what we hear with the outer ear is not what we will pick up with the inner ear. And it is the interior experience that will illumine and elucidate the experience of the outer senses.

...and the beauty and obscurity of those other divine fragments which are struggling side by side with you, and form the race to which you belong.

We must come to understand the evolutionary process of ourselves as well as "the beauty and obscurity of those other divine fragments which are struggling side by side with you, and form the race to which you belong." We are all of us divine fragments, little pieces of the puzzle that (seemingly) have fallen away from the divine unity. However ignorantly we may behave, however tiresome we can be, we are yet divine fragments. We are never anything else. The realization that we are parts of the Whole, and the resulting respect for the other parts we call "fellow-men," is a part of the *swadhyaya*, self-study, recommended by Patanjali. Self-study entails the utilization of all these interior faculties to understand the growth and the meaning of our individuality.

By understanding ourselves we shall accordingly come to understand indeed "the beauty and obscurity of those other divine fragments." Notice that the Master puts "beauty" before "obscurity" because the real quality of all beings is beauty, the obscuration being only a temporary condition, a mere appearance. Yet we must be aware of both, though in perspective. This is not a matter of superficial verbal affirmation; this must be an actual seeing of the beauty and the obscurity both of ourselves and of those around us.

Seek it by study of the laws of being, the laws of nature, the laws of the supernatural.

This is because we are going to use a definite methodology, and to be effective that methodology has to conform to the laws of nature, specifically those regarding evolution. For example, in meditation we sit upright, rather than lie down, because we know the subtle currents flow upward to the higher centers of awareness in the brain when we sit upright, and disperse throughout the body when we lie down so we go to sleep. This is also why we pay attention to diet and certain modes of behavior. We know that they affect the subtle energies involved in the evolution of consciousness.

Basically, we must slip through the net by studying the net. We must understand the way the world conditions us, so that we can become deconditioned. We must understand the weights that are put on us so we can divest ourselves of them.

Real religion is very sophisticated in its understanding of nature, the components of nature and the subtle forces of nature. It is far more sophisticated than any material science can ever be because material science is concerned exclusively with external phenomena, which are the most superficial of phenomena. We also have to know the deep things of ourselves to know the inner laws of our makeup and how they work. This is why in religion that works there is more emphasis placed on the invisible than on the visible, more exploration of the unseen forces than of the seen. That is because the unseen forces are much nearer to the consciousness that is our real Self.

"Seek it by the study of the laws of being." In other words, we must seek to comprehend how we come into manifestation, for once we know that we can begin our return to the Unmanifest.

...and seek it by making the profound obeisance of the soul to the dim star that burns within.

"Seek it by the study of the laws of... the supernatural," counsels the Master, because the roots of all lesser laws are there in the spirit, "the dim star that burns within." Consequently we must come to know the laws of the spirit and scrupulously follow them. The ways of spirit are the true Law of God, and must be adhered to absolutely in all conditions and at all times. There is nothing free-form here. It is precise and it is certainly absolute. There are neither exceptions nor modifications. This is why discipline and perfect observance of spiritual laws are the only real way to freedom.

Steadily, as you watch and worship, its light will grow stronger. Then you may know you have found the beginning of the way.

"Seek it by making the profound obeisance of the soul to the dim star that burns within." The whole of the soul must be offered there, must bow before that dim light within. It is very dim in the beginning; sometimes we cannot even see it at first. But "steadily, as you watch and worship, its light will grow stronger." This is real worship. Worship is not making offerings of external things, but of consciousness: ourselves. When we sit and ignore all else but that, and we let that light alone lead or draw us to itself, that is the ultimate worship.

As the Master says, that light, that inner star, may at first be very dim, but perseverance reveals its blazing glory, but as we watch and worship interiorly we shall come to realize that it is the Living Presence of God. Therefore meditation should be approached with reverence, for by means of it we are placing ourselves in the presence of God.

And when you have found the end its light will suddenly become the infinite light.

Spiritual leaders in India are constantly being plied with a "spiritual" cliche that after a while comes to be most annoying. It goes like this: "We have visited so many mahatmas (great souls) yet we do not obtain peace of mind." Of course this is really excuse-making for their lack of spiritual progress, and implies that the mahatmas are at fault for their non-attainment.

The first time this was tossed out at me I batted the ball back by answering: "You are only looking at one part of it: what you should be *doing* to obtain peace of mind. Now let's look at what you ought to *quit doing* in your life, so that you can get peace of mind." Hey, presto! The questioning ceased instantly.

And anyway: nowhere in the scriptures is it said that peace of mind can be gained by visiting mahatmas. Rather, it is said that following the wisdom of mahatmas brings peace of mind, and that entails meditation and moral principles.

There is no use sitting in the hog wallow complaining: "I have been spraying perfume all day long, so why does it still smell bad?" We have to get up and move out of the filth. We must learn what to cut out of our life as well as what to add to our life.

21. Look for the flower to bloom in the silence that follows the storm: not till then.

It shall grow, it will shoot up, it will make branches and leaves and form buds, while the storm continues, while the battle lasts. But not till the whole personality of the man is dissolved and melted—not until it is held by the divine fragment which has created it, as a mere subject for grave experiment and experience—not until the whole nature has yielded and become subject unto its higher self, can the bloom open. Then will come a calm such as comes in a tropical country after the heavy rain, when Nature works so swiftly that one may see her action. Such a calm will come to the harassed spirit. And in the deep silence the mysterious event will occur which will prove that the way has been found. Call it by what name you will, it is a voice that speaks where there is none to speak—it is a messenger that comes, a messenger without form or substance; or it is the flower of

the soul that has opened. It cannot be described by any metaphor. But it can be felt after, looked for, and desired, even amid the raging of the storm. The silence may last a moment of time or it may last a thousand years. But it will end. Yet you will carry its strength with you. Again and again the battle must be fought and won. It is only for an interval that Nature can be still.

Look for the flower to bloom in the silence that follows the storm: not till then.

The result does not come while we are still working at something, but only when the work is completed. In India the yogis frequently say: "Making, making, made!" Buddhists recite a sutra that can colloquially be rendered as: "Going, going, gone!" expressing the same idea. Even a statue is not completed until the last stroke is done and the chisel and mallet are laid aside. Only when the storm is over, duality has vanished, all coming and going has ceased and all change has been transcended, will the flower bloom in the silence.

If we pick up a cat by the tail, it is going to start scratching and biting us. Praying to God, asking that the cat stop, will do no good, nor will all the affirmative philosophy in the world help us. We have to let go of the cat's tail. So as long as we have the cat by the tail, as long as we are still holding on to our ego, to the material side of our existence, it is going to continue clawing us. That is its very nature, so why would we expect anything else?

My paternal grandfather was a typical Victorian father, and was used to his second eldest daughter, Elizabeth, pouring his tea for him. Once when she was not there, he took the teapot himself and began to pour from it. When the cup was nearly full, he snapped: "There, Liz!" The tea went right on flowing up to the top of the cup. Again he said: "There, Liz!" And, of course, it kept going on. "There, Liz!" he repeated. Then, as the cup overflowed, he shouted: "There, Liz, drat you!" Everyone else at the table began laughing, and he realized that he himself was doing the pouring. In the same way, it is no use to ask God or anyone else to stop it. We are doing it all ourselves. The stopping is completely up to us.

Will nothing worthwhile happen until the storm is over? Much indeed will happen during and because of the storm. The Master says:

It shall grow, it will shoot up, it will make branches and leaves and form buds, while the storm continues, while the battle lasts.

We are in no way wasting our time as we are engaging in the interior work of transformation. The lotus of enlightenment will grow, shoot up, and produce branches, leaves, and buds. And when that is over the lotus will bloom.

But not till the whole personality of the man is dissolved and melted—not until it is held by the divine fragment which has created it, as a mere subject for grave experiment and experience—not until the whole nature has yielded and become subject unto its higher self, can the bloom open.

The "divine fragment" is us: our immortal spirit. We are a spark of light in the great Ocean of Light that is God. And we put on the costume of the various bodies and that which we call "personality" in order to enter into relative existence and thereby develop the capacity to share in God's infinite consciousness. (Please see *Robe of Light* for more regarding this.) And we have let our personality and its powers run amok like a chariot dragged along by runaway horses. That which was meant to be an instrument which we could use through the force of an illumined will has instead taken over and created utter chaos in us who should be the masters rather than the mastered.

As the Master says, we have created all the facets of our personality—no one else. In time, though, all this that we have gathered around us must be melted and dissolved, returned to the primal light from whence it came. Until that is done, we cannot possibly attain any significant degree of spiritual enlightenment: enlightenment and freedom being the same thing. As long as the shackles are on us, it is silly for us to say that we are free.

Why did we create this personality and its vehicles? "For grave experiment and experience." This matter of evolution is no superficial game, it is extremely serious indeed. For it is a matter of life and death in the highest and most profound sense. Our purpose was to go out from God finite, and to return to God infinite, but we have become locked into this relative identity instead of using it to realize its full potential so we can transcend it and go on to a higher form, eventually transcending the highest form to unite our consciousness with that of God. Not only have we become confined to our personality-costume, through identity with it we have created karma which keeps drawing us back into incarnation again and again.

We should have manifested each particular form (evolutionary level) only once and then passed upward to the next higher form, having realized the full potential of the discarded form. We consider children stupid if they have to repeat the same grade over and over again, but we think that it is perfectly all right for us to have hundreds of human births. As I pointed out sometime back, it is not flattering to tell someone: "You are an old soul," when we understand what it implies. A real compliment would be to say to a person practicing spiritual discipline: "You are a very new soul."

By our own efforts we have to dissolve and melt the personality-vehicle so that we can go on higher. "Not until the whole nature has yielded and become subject unto its higher Self, can the bloom open." In other words, the spirit must dominate, must rule from the first to the last. If the higher Self does not do that, then there is no use to look for the bloom. We should not wonder at our lack of attainment. We need to look carefully within and see who is occupying the throne of our inmost heart, for only one can sit there at a time. We have to decide who will sit there: the ego or the true Self. They cannot share the dominion, for they are mutually exclusive. Jesus said that we cannot serve two masters (Matthew 6:24). Our single master must be our higher Self. Then the sacred lotus of spirit will bloom.

The Master is telling us to keep at it, to keep on working, looking neither to the right nor to the left, but to press onward, ever onward. "Turn not to the right hand nor to the left" (Proverbs 4:27). And above all, he is telling us not to go looking for something that it is not even the time to attain. So the Master is saying to not go looking out of season for the bloom of the spirit.

Then will come a calm such as comes in a tropical country after the heavy rain, when Nature works so swiftly that one may see her action.

The Master is referring to the Asian monsoons after which vegetation grows so rapidly that it seems to be growing before the eyes of the observer.

There is another reason why the monsoon is used as a symbol. Unlike our rainy seasons in the West, in which the sky is continually overcast, in the Orient during monsoon season the sky is usually completely clear. This is because the monsoons blow in rapidly. (I learned this at the cost of a few instant soakings when I was in Calcutta during the monsoon season.) You can go out of the house and find the sky as blue and clear as on any dry summer day. As you proceed along the street, everything is just fine, and then in a moment torrential rains pour down on you, soaking you in a matter of seconds. If you can, you take refuge under some type of shelter and wait. Just as suddenly the rains stop, the sun shines, and the sky is as empty of clouds as before. The clouds have been either totally emptied of rain or have been blown onward. The clouds represent the forces of karma which must be either utterly exhausted or somehow transcended. Also, when the rain is over it is absolutely over, and the resulting calm is also absolute. This is because the relative–therefore delusive–personality is dissolved like the clouds, never to return.

Such a calm will come to the harassed spirit. And in the deep silence the mysterious event will occur which will prove that the way has been found.

The spirit is indeed harassed, having been trapped in the whirling energies of ever-changing bodies and minds through aeons, each body-mind a wolf that seized and attempted to devour the spirit, to arrogate its immortal nature and life unto itself whose essential nature was mortality and death.

"And in the deep silence the mysterious event will occur which will prove that the way has been found." The mysterious event is as ineffable as That which it reveals, so I will make no attempt to describe or define it. But when it happens it will be known for what it is.

Call it by what name you will, it is a voice that speaks where there is none to speak…

The Master is not going to describe it, because if it was describable it would be something in the realm of relativity and therefore within the reach of language. This also indicates to us that we are going toward a permanent condition, not just a state of momentary quiet. A crowd can be quieted, but it can erupt into noise a moment later. What we must do is empty ourselves so that there is no one there to "speak." This is the only condition that will produce real calm and peace.

It has already been mentioned that Sri Ramakrishna often spoke of the salt doll that went to measure the ocean, but when the salt doll got in the ocean it melted and there was no one to come back to tell how deep the ocean was. In other words, the egoistic idea "I will go measure, and then come back and tell others" is dissolved. Dr. Jacques Weintrob (Vijayananda) told me that when the then-well-known writer Arthur Koestler was in India he came to Varanasi to see Anandamayi Ma. While waiting to have an interview, he began a conversation with Vijayananda. At one point he asked: "When you become enlightened and liberated will you come back and help others to do the same?" Vijayananda said: "Your question has no meaning. If someone is asleep and dreams he is in prison with many others, does he say: 'When I wake up I am going to come back here and get these others out of prison'?"

The Buddhist Master Ho Tai taught the same thing in a more objective way. When asked what enlightenment was, he put down the large sack he was carrying. When asked what the objectification of enlightenment was, he picked it back up and walked on. There was nothing to be said. In silence was the message.

...it is a messenger that comes, a messenger without form or substance; or it is the flower of the soul that has opened. It cannot be described by any metaphor. But it can be felt after, looked for, and desired, even amid the raging of the storm.

By "feeling" the Master means intuiting, not emoting. That is, we can intuit it and feel that it is real, feel that its attainment is possible. We can know that it is there. We may not know exactly what is there, but we can know that it is there, as a blind person can sense the presence of another. So we can have this dim feeling of "something," if nothing more. We can look for and desire it, literally yearn for it, even while the storm is raging. For it is one of the things that will help us get over the storm.

The silence may last a moment of time or it may last a thousand years. But it will end.

Remember that Ho Tai picked up his sack and walked away. That is, the "moment" will not be the end, rather it will be the beginning of an entirely new mode of consciousness, and therefore of life.

The eternal moment comes to us according to the distinctive character of the tides of our inner life. If we are waiting and ready for that moment, then we will cycle up to a higher mode of being. But if we are too busy looking at the scenery or lazing around, taking it easy for the moment, we will not only miss it, we will not even know that it came.

One of the worst delusions we can have about spiritual life is that we have unlimited time to "get on board." It is indeed true that we have eternity to dawdle in, but it is not true that the door is always open. For some the door opens for quite a long time, and for others it opens for a short time and then closes. But close it eventually does if we do not pass through it. And for most people the door then remains closed until a future birth.

Many times I have seen people wasting their life, assuring themselves that in a few months or years they would knuckle down and seriously begin their search. In each case they lost their opportunity for this lifetime. And since we reap what we sow, in a future life when they do begin to seek, the door will be denied them—or be completely unknown to them for some time—perhaps for that life as well.

Although it does not quite fit in here, I want to explain a principle of spiritual life that everyone should know: Whatever it might be in our life that causes us to turn away from spiritual life in order to possess or retain it, that very thing will be taken from us, and we will then be without it and without spiritual life as well. We shall drift in the sky of life like a broken cloud for the rest of our incarnation and perhaps for a few future ones. Over and over I have seen people give up their spiritual life for the sake of getting or keeping some thing, person or relationship that demanded their full commitment. In every case they lost what they were grasping for, and never turned back to the Way of Life.

Let the wise be warned: we must never sacrifice our spiritual life for anything. Not only will it be a foolish choice, we will either never gain it or we will lose it altogether. The moment of decision does not last forever. It comes and goes from life to life.

Yet you will carry its strength with you.

For those who do grasp the moment, the Master gives the assurance that although it may pass, "yet you will carry its strength with you." All along the way, as we spiral upward, we reach plateaus from which we usually do not slip back.

Again and again the battle must be fought and won.

Many times we hear people complain that they keep struggling with the same problems over and over again. What they do not realize is that each time they are struggling with them on a different level, for the roots of ignorance strike deep, passing through many layers of our being.

It is only for an interval that Nature can be still.

By Nature is meant the whole range of existence, up to the highest worlds. And it is in those moments of true silence that the most progress can be made, progress that will be of permanent effect. Eventually we will be able to pass into the perfect silence forever, but until then we must be content with, and ready for, those rare moments when the tides of duality are in abeyance. To reach those moments we must enter into the core of our being, for there alone the Silence is found.

Have we now finished? Not at all! The Master now assures us that:

These written above are the first of the rules which are written on the walls of the Hall of Learning. Those that ask shall have. Those that desire to read shall read. Those who desire to learn shall learn. Peace be with you.

PART TWO

Out of the silence that is peace a resonant voice shall arise. And this voice will say, It is not well; thou hast reaped, now thou must sow. And knowing this voice to be the silence itself thou wilt obey.

Thou who art now a disciple, able to stand, able to hear, able to see, able to speak, who hast conquered desire and attained to self-knowledge, who hast seen thy soul in its bloom and recognized it, and hear the voice of the silence, go thou to the Hall of Learning and read what is written there for thee.

Out of the silence that is peace...

It is not the mere silence of no sound, just as keeping silence does not mean to simply not speak. There are those who are noisier when they "keep silence" than when they do not. How well do I remember what a joke some people's "day of silence" would be. I could know it was their day of silence because they banged everything they picked up, stomped across the floor when they walked, and slammed every door they closed. If they did a simple thing like the dishes it sounded like the Charge of the Light Brigade. It was obvious they just could not endure silence. And instead of staying home and being quiet, they would go around people with a piece of paper pinned on them saying: "This is my day of silence." Then they would gesture wildly and make odd noises rather than speak: wasting more energy than if they had shouted and jumped around. One woman would go into a temper spell if her gyrations and huffings were not understood.

Therefore one spiritual leader in India said: "Avoid at all costs those who while pretending to keep silence write notes and make gestures." As Anandamayi Ma said, if we just do not want to speak that is one thing; but if we want to keep silence, that is another.

So the silence that is peace is something more than just the absence of sound. The great Staretz Adrian of Novo-Divyevo in Nanuet, New York, said that from childhood he perceived real spiritual atmosphere and presence as a pervading silence in the midst of all movement and sound. He said that he especially found it in church services; that although singing and movement were going on he experienced an utter stillness which he intuitively knew was the essence of spiritual life: a stillness that could be found in the heart of movement, not in the absence of movement.

His words bring to mind this statement of Krishna in the Gita: "He who perceives inaction in action and action in inaction—such a man is wise among men, steadfast in yoga and doing all action" (Bhagavad Gita 4:18). There is movement in stillness and stillness that is in movement. That is why in the temples of India when it is time for worship all of a sudden everything begins to bang and clang: gongs are beaten, conch shells are sounded, and bells are rung. Usually many people are singing loudly. And yet, if you examine your inner mind you will discover that in that moment you have entered into perfect silence. This is a secret that only the East comprehends. To attain silence we need not stop sound, rather we need to move into That which is at the center of sound. (Once more: see *Soham Yoga: The Yoga of the Self.*)

Saint Silouan of Athos wrote that people have lived in deserts and caves supposedly alone, and yet have had the whole world with them in their minds. In contrast was Saint John of Kronstadt, who was never physically alone except for a hour or two a day, yet was always alone. When he was in the midst of thousands of people pressing around him, wanting to touch him and speak to him, it was evident that he was absolutely alone, that nothing of the pandemonium around him was touching his mind. He was alone with God even then.

> Alone with God, the world forbidden,
> Alone with God, O blest retreat!
> Alone with God, and in Him hidden,
> To hold with Him communion sweet.

...a resonant voice shall arise.

In the Silence there is a voice, that silent (still) subtle (small) impulse which is the very root of "word" and therefore The Word itself. It cannot be at all expressed in human terms, for it is far beyond the senses and ordinary experience. And it only speaks when there is none other to speak.

And this voice will say, It is not well; thou hast reaped, now thou must sow.

Being oriented to egoic gratification, even in spiritual life, we have the idea that we need only enjoy our attainments, revel in them, and congratulate ourselves on having at last "made it." But the Voice of Truth tells us that such "is not well." Rather: "Thou hast reaped, now thou must sow." This is very interesting, for we usually think that reaping is the end of it all. We reason that we are in the world to reap our karmas, and when that is done, all has been done: rebirth will be ended, all bonds dissolved. But the inmost voice says otherwise. There is more to be done.

And knowing this voice to be the silence itself thou wilt obey.

We will not wonder whether the voice is right. In that state we will know it is Truth itself, the truth of our own Self, and the Self of our Self that speaks. And we will obey. This is the path of the disciple. It is not rhapsodic talk about "masters" that is the path. Rather, discipline is the path—discipline that is an act of our illumined will, not a passive acquiescence to an outside influence.

Thou who art now a disciple, able to stand, able to hear, able to see, able to speak, who hast conquered desire and attained to self-knowledge, who hast seen thy soul in its bloom and recognized, and heard the voice of the silence, go thou to the Hall of Learning and read what is written there for thee.

Those who have truly attained to any degree of spiritual progress do not want to be teachers, but aspire to be perfect learners. To help us, then, the Master is going to outline just what the traits of worthy disciples are.

Able to stand. That is, able to be established in one spot, unshaken in spiritual awareness, able to endure, possessing firmness and stability on all levels, which also implies *definition* on all levels.

Able to hear. In other words, possessing the ear of the spirit. ("He that hath ears to hear, let him hear" Matthew 11:15.)

Able to see with the single "eye" of enlightenment. "The light of the body is the eye: if therefore thine eye be single, thy whole body shall be full of light" (Matthew 6:22).

All these descriptive statements imply something: namely that before this time we are not able to stand, to hear, and to see. Of course we could do so on the lower level of existence, and we can entrench ourselves in ignorance very easily. We can hear all kinds of foolishness, see all kinds of foolishness, and speak all kinds of foolishness. All that we do out of ignorance is but a mockery of the real powers we should (and already innately do) have.

Able to speak, possessing the Power of Word. This is perhaps the most important of all, for it is listed last as the capstone, the finishing touch. Perhaps the most commonly heard complaint from those dwelling in the darkness of their egos is that of not having their prayers answered or that God does not hear their prayers. Of course they are right. God does *not* hear their prayers because God is a spirit, and they do not pray with the spirit, but with the ego-mind. Only the yogi-disciple has opened the inner mouth with which effective prayer or affirmation can be made. The non-yogi disciple may speak much, but on the inner planes he is a mute.

Who has conquered desire and attained to self-knowledge. Notice the cause and effect implied here. Desire is an impediment to Self-knowledge. How can that be? Because desire is based on and affirms the delusion that external objects can produce the internal experience of happiness, peace or fulfillment. As long as desire is allowed to motivate our behavior we are willfully blinding ourself to the truth that everything is within us, that we can have nothing else, and that spiritually we are sufficient unto ourselves.

Once we attain Self-knowledge, is it the end as most suppose? No. Beyond Self-knowledge is God-knowledge, beyond Self-realization is God-realization—although in a mysterious way the two are one. Once we have established our consciousness in the little deity of our Self, then we have to learn to expand into the infinite Deity—whom the German philosophers have called the Over-Soul and whom the sages of India have named Parabrahman, Paramatman and Parameshwara.

You, O disciple, are one who has "attained to Self-knowledge, who hast seen thy soul in its bloom and recognized it, and heard the voice of the silence." This is no small thing: to have perceived the evolution of the spirit and by means of that perception to have heard the Word spoken in the depths of your soul. Yet it is in no way the end. Having attained to a high degree of knowledge, you are now capable of learning much, much more.

Go thou to the Hall of Learning and read what is written there for thee. Written into the very fabric of the creation are those principles or archetypal patterns that we think of as "laws." Many of them are related to spiritual life—spiritual evolution. So if we would truly ascend beyond the bonds of all limitations of consciousness we will carefully ascertain those laws and follow them scrupulously.

It is very easy to be fooled by the ego and our inexperience into thinking that we have attained everything when we have only just begun. I once read an autobiographical sketch of a woman who claimed that when she began spiritual life she attained cosmic consciousness in two weeks and then quickly went on to higher things. Not likely! Once in India I heard a man speaking to Triguna Sen, a friend of mine, about getting an interview with Sri Anandamayi Ma. "I don't need any advice on spiritual life from her," he confided, "because I already have attained self-realization. I'm not concerned about that." Triguna was visibly amazed. "Well, then, what do you want to talk to Mother about?" "I want to ask her if there is anything beyond perfection that I should be looking for." Hearing this exchange, I could not help but remember a letter written to Swami Bhaktivedanta, the founder of the Hare Krishna movement. A man wrote that he had joined some of Swamiji's disciples in singing the Hare Krishna mantra one afternoon in Central Park. He had felt very uplifted and inwardly elated by doing so, and he wanted to know if that meant he had become enlightened. Bhaktivedanta replied: "When you eat a big meal do you need to ask someone if you are full? Keep on chanting Hare Krishna." Simple profound truth.

1. Stand aside in the coming battle, and though thou fightest be not thou the warrior.

In the first section we were exhorted to be completely active: "kill out ambition,... kill out desire of life,... kill out desire of comfort,... work as those who work, work,... seek,... desire,... look...." So much to do! In light of that we would naturally assume that we are going to be told more of the same. But not so. This time we must step aside. Yet not because it is going to be a time of peace, for the entire instruction is: "Stand aside in the coming battle."

There is a battle coming, and we should step aside? It seems confusing, but there is an incident in the *Mahabharata* that may help us. After years of attempts at peace between the Kauravas and the Pandavas, it was seen that war was inevitable because the Kauravas wanted it. Sides were being drawn up. Arjuna the great yogi was going to be the leader of the Pandava side and the evil Duryodhana would head the Kauravas. All the rulers of India had gathered for the negotiations, so Arjuna and Duryodhana were going to each one and asking which side they would fight on. Most said that they would fight on the side of the Kauravas. (The Kauravas outnumbered the Pandavas more than twenty to one when the battle finally took place.) Last of all they went to Krishna, whose army was one of the largest in India. Duryodhana hated Krishna, whom he had several times tried to kill. So he was sure that Krishna would side with the Pandavas. Arjuna was of the same opinion. But when they put the question, to the astonishment of both Krishna said: "There is my army and there is me. One of you can have my army, and the other can have me: but I will not fight." Duryodhana was chagrined. Surely Arjuna would choose the army and he would be left with Krishna whom he loathed and hoped to kill. Arjuna did not hesitate. "Duryodhana can have your army," he said, "but you must drive my chariot, even though you do not fight." And so it was agreed. Krishna did not fight, but drove the chariot of Arjuna, and the Pandavas won, for: "Wherever there is Krishna, Yoga's Lord, wherever is Arjuna the bowman, there will forever be splendor, victory, wealth and righteousness" (Bhagavad Gita 18:78). That is, where there is the Supreme Reality and one who heeds Its wisdom, there is victory assured.

So the Master is not telling us to be negatively passive, but rather to identify with pure spirit, the eternal witness of all that takes place in relativity. Creation and its "story" is the dance of the Holy Spirit Mother before the Only-begotten Father-Son. When we identify with the dance it sweeps us along in its tides, but when we identify with the unmoving Consciousness of God we are the masters, the lords of the dance.

Stand aside in the coming battle, and though thou fightest be not thou the warrior. Amazing! We are to fight and not be the warrior. Yet it is not contradictory if we realize that it is the Eternal that does all things within time, that there is only one Doer, and that is God: including the god within (and which is) us. It is a matter of identity. Act, but do not act. Be out of the picture while in the picture. This is no easy matter. Nor is it just talk. No theory here: only Gnosis (Jnana) will do the needful.

We must understand that everything we are experiencing is simply the movement around us of the divine light, that it is teaching us, showing us the truth that it is an illusion, but *not* a lie: that it is a "training film" of Wisdom. After all, the word "gate" is not a gate, but we do not refuse to use it, for it gives us the awareness of an actual gate. In the same way the Divine Illusion leads us to the Divine Reality.

Our problem is that we have fallen into the Illusion and identified with it fully, forgetting the truth of our nature as consciousness, as spirit. "Virtual reality" in which we can electronically experience things without really doing them is modern, but that is what we have already been doing through countless incarnations. And we have forgotten the truth about ourselves and come to believe only in the truth of our sense perceptions, which are illusions, and suffer as a consequence. For if we do not learn from them, we do not get the message. And we never will until we pull back, stand aside and observe.

This is really essential, and this is very, very, *very* hard to do, because naturally we want to meddle with the movie and control it, not realizing that it is only going to unfold as it is going to unfold: that we are just pinpoints in a vast sea of creative power which is meant to teach us and develop in us the capacity for ever-increasing modes of consciousness. And it is only through perfection of consciousness that we can truly deal with the world around and within us. We must stop thinking that the mirror image is our real face. We should use the mirror, but we must not lose sight of the fact that it is a mirror and not "the thing itself." We must come to identify with spirit and use the fundamental instrument of consciousness: the creative will.

The creation dances, we do not dance. But it appears that we do. We must not succumb to that appearance. Once when seeing a temple flag waving in the wind, a Zen disciple asked his master: "Which is moving, the flag or the wind?" The master replied: "The mind is moving." We "fight" through the application of our will, but it is the creation that responds and is the real "warrior."

So we do fight—but we are not the fighter. It is all by "remote control." We must learn to "do" things as God does them.

The first time we went to the Hall of Learning (in Part One) the Master let us think we were the doer, because he understood that we could not yet comprehend the truth of this—and if we did we would most likely dislike and reject it. We would no doubt be like the famous muppet, Fozzie Bear in the program *Here Come the Puppets*. He looked down and called out in alarm. When Kermit came to see what was the trouble, Fozzie grabbed him and yelled: "Don't look down!" Then he said in a loud whisper: "There is somebody underneath me." And he looked down and shouted, "No, don't look! There's somebody underneath you, too!" "Of course. We're Muppets and those people are working us," Kermit explained. Fozzie put his hands on his head and protested: "I just can't relate to that concept!" We would have reacted the same way.

Our minds have to be evolved enough to handle the higher metaphysical facts. Otherwise we misunderstand or reject them. Some people simply shatter when confronted with the truth. And then they run. Even Vivekananda, when he first came to Sri Ramakrishna, used to mock the idea that all was God. But in time he learned, and spent the rest of his life teaching multitudes that all is God. We, too, must ripen, and the Master knew that. First he urged us to act, and now he tells us to stand aside, just as our parents send us to school in hope that one day we will graduate and quit going to school. As we move from level to level in our growth there will be corresponding changes in our outlook and approach to life in all its aspects. It is like the Buddhist Master that asked a philosophical question of a disciple. When the disciple answered, the Master said: "Yes, that is right." The next day he asked the same question, and upon receiving the same answer responded: "No, that is wrong." "But yesterday you said my answer was right," the disciple protested. "Yesterday it was right; today it is wrong," the Master told him. Was he being capricious? No. In the meantime the disciple had grown enough to hold a more accurate view. And chances are the "right" answer switched back and forth several times before he attained that state in which there are no answers at all, for there are no more questions or even the possibility of questions.

It is time to stop Doing and start Being.

2. Look for the warrior and let him fight in thee.

Perhaps before beginning to comment on the verse as a whole it would be good to look at what the Master means by "him." Although the Master uses the singular term "him" in this section, two entities are spoken of, the singular form being used for two reasons: 1) you must first find one before finding the other, and 2) they are one in essence.

The mystery (at least to the limited human mind) of diversity in unity and unity in diversity, especially in relation to the duality/unity of God and individual spirits, has exercised the minds of higher philosophers of all ages and traditions. The wise have concluded that the "how" of this is simply beyond human comprehension, but they are unanimous in stating that this truth can be directly perceived through development of the consciousness within each one of us. In other words, the Reality that is the real nature of consciousness, finite and infinite, can be known through inner, mystical experience.

It is imperative, then, that we keep in mind throughout the Master's exposition that both God and man are being spoken of. Knowledge of God is impossible without the prerequisite of Self-knowledge. The individual must come to know himself as finite, eternal pure consciousness (spirit), drawing its existence from, and ever within, the infinite eternal pure consciousness that is God. Although the Master's immediate message is the necessity for Self-realization, he is assuming that God-realization will be its natural corollary.

Look for the warrior and let him fight in thee.

The first point made by this simple statement is that the coming activity in the spirit is not going to be automatic. One of the illusions cherished by us in our egoic laziness is the idea that the day will come when we will spontaneously do the right things and accomplish what we should. We like this idea of spontaneity because it implies the lack of any effort on our part whatsoever. In other words, we do not want to row up the river, we want to drift down on the current. But this is an impossibility, especially for persons on the human rung of the evolutionary ladder.

To escape from the bondage of ignorance which prevails in this world, effort is needed until we draw our last breath. The strength for the effort is indeed drawn from the reservoir of God's power, but the very drawing itself can sometimes be a labor for us. Every step on the path to reunion with God must of necessity be a conscious act of will.

Many of those who observe us walking this path begin screaming about brainwashing, mind control, mental dominance, undue influence and loss of freedom of thought and will. These rants are the "tools of the trade" of those who tread the very path upon which they accuse us of following. *They themselves* are embarked on the way of enslavement and destruction.

For it is the world that:

   brainwashes us into acceptance of its illusions,

   controls our minds in an endeavor to keep us from awakening
and escaping its bondage,

demands that our minds be occupied continually with the struggle for survival and the distractions of earthly life,

warps our mind and makes it a complete slave to externality,

and renders us incapable of thinking or willing independently or contrary to the currents of earthly life.

Moreover, those who are the slaves of this world and who to a greater or lesser degree consciously serve it as their master, work the same destruction upon their fellow human beings. Therefore when they see anyone attempting to escape from their nets of deception they begin accusing them of the very things which they are perpetrating on humanity. They express disgust, even horror and disbelief at every practice which works to free us from their domination, and try to convince others that it is we who are working their dark works.

However much the opposition may bellow, the disciple must (and does) follow the path of conscious choice. All along the way, the lorelei forces of ignorance call out to entice us with promises of ease, peace, and rest if only we will step from the path and begin to drift with them. How enticing it is to the weary warrior at times! Our egos may clothe the desire for surrender in high-sounding terms of philosophy, but cowardly surrender it still remains.

The path of the disciple is not a weekend excursion, and those of shallow and short-lived motivation should not step upon it lest in time they fall to their greater destruction. I have seen people push their way into situations for which they were not spiritually prepared (especially into monastic life or positions of spiritual supervision or authority). In each instance they did not just fall, they plunged into the depths of negativity and inner destruction.

But it is assumed by the Master that those whom he addresses have determined to follow the path to its very end and beyond. So he exhorts them to look for the warrior. For those who are outward-turned it will be a search through the labyrinth of external existence, both material and psychic. Even a somewhat awakened soul may pass lifetimes plunging into the depths and scaling the heights of the material and psychic worlds seeking for power, seeking for knowledge, looking for that "warrior" which can win the victory over ignorance and bring enlightenment. The world could not hold the volumes that might be written to record these desperate searches, searches that by their very nature are doomed to fail. Why? Because they are searches outward rather than inward. There are two incidents that illustrate this very well. One is a kind of humorous parable and one is a true life experience. As might be expected, both are from India.

In earlier times (not really so long ago) devout Hindus used to walk the "pilgrim's trail" which went in a great circle around the entire Indian subcontinent and connected a series of centers of great spiritual power. There was a man who spent some years on this ambitious pilgrimage, and everywhere he went he would buy an image of the presiding deity of that particular holy place. Finally, toward the end of his pilgrimage, he was staggering along carrying on his shoulders two large wooden boxes filled with holy images. Whenever he would stop for the night, he would spread them out, do worship to each in turn, and after several hours sleep. When he awoke in the morning he would again perform worship of all for some hours, then wrap the images up, put them in the box, and labor onwards.

One day a wandering monk observed all this and said to him: "Why do you bother to worship all these deities? Why don't you just worship the most powerful god, and then you will get the benefits you would have from worshipping such a multitude." Then he quickly walked on. The man began to ponder how he could determine which was the most powerful deity. Not being very bright, he hit upon an interesting decision: he would take an image in either hand and strike them together as hard as he could. The image that did not break would be the most powerful deity. So he spent the next couple of hours smashing his images against one another. Since most of them were made of clay or brittle stone, and only one of them was made of metal, in time he was left with that alone. Happy that he had at last found which was the most powerful deity, he tucked it in his bundle of clothing and bedding, gave the wooden box a kick, and went on his way.

After reaching home, he expressed to his parents the desire to have his own household, so they arranged a marriage for him and in time he and his wife lived in their own house. Near the house he constructed a small hut in which he installed the surviving image and worshipped it daily, often boasting to his neighbors about his success in finding the most powerful of the gods. Understanding that meditation is important, he also began to meditate before the image after having first performed worship and, as is the custom in India, giving offerings of food to the deity.

Once as he was meditating, he heard sounds from the altar, and opened his eyes to see that the cat had knocked over the image and was eating the food. Rather than being enraged, he was delighted. Obviously the cat was a more powerful god than the one he had been bothering with! So he began to worship the cat and every day he put out food on the altar, the cat would eat it, and he would sit and meditate, visualizing in his heart the form of the cat.

After some time of this worship, he happened to see his wife shooing the cat away from the house. She whacked it with her broom and kicked it with her foot. The cat ran away, but the man ran and bowed before his wife. "You are greater than all the gods," he told her, "even more powerful than the cat god." So from then on he worshipped his wife. He would have her sit on the altar, and he would meditate on her.

It did not take long for her to get tired of this foolishness, so one day she refused to come and be worshipped. This made him so angry that he picked up a stick and threatened to beat her if she did not cooperate. Off she ran to the hut-temple.

As he put down the stick, he came to the realization that he must be more powerful than his wife, and therefore the greater god. He went and shooed her out of the hut, sat himself on the altar, and began to meditate upon himself. And, it is said, he attained enlightenment, for the true light is of course within.

A friend of mine from eastern India (Bengal) in his younger life had been a medical doctor with the British Army, though he was himself Indian. "I was a real sahib," he laughed, "well booted, well suited, well hatted, and with my hair all cut and oiled like an Englishman." Considering himself a man of science, he had no time for the "superstitions" of Hinduism or any other religion. All his attention was centered on his career and the support of his wife and their two children, a girl six years old and a boy two years old.

One morning upon arising he noticed that the children were not there. When he asked his wife about their absence, she carelessly answered: "Oh, they are off with their guru." He was literally thunderstruck. In the Himalayan foothill region where he was then living it was not uncommon for children to wander off with the roaming monks who were continually passing through on pilgrimage. He began to shout at his wife: "Guru and kidnapper are the same thing! How could you let them go off like this?" His wife was not affected by his furor, and told him: "They only went out a short time ago, so why don't you go after them?" This he did, though only half dressed.

He went rushing along looking into every street and alley, hoping to get a glimpse of his children. As he emerged from the end of the street at the edge of the town, he turned a corner and encountered an amazing spectacle. Walking along the road was an unusually tall Hindu monk dressed in the traditional orange robes. An immense beard covered the front of his chest, and long hair covered his back. Impressive as his appearance was, the doctor was most struck by another element of the scene. Two dozen or more children were walking along behind the swami in perfect order and silence: two elements usually missing in children. His two-year-old son was holding on to the swami's robe so he could keep up.

Not knowing what he was going to do or say, the doctor stepped out in front of the swami. "You have my children," was what he said. The swami nodded. "Yes, do you want them back?" "No, they seem to be quite well with you," was the automatic reply. Again the swami nodded. "Then come and see me tonight at my ashram." Having received instructions as to the ashram's location, the doctor went back home in a daze, dressed completely and went to his work.

That evening he went to visit the swami. "You are a medical doctor," said the swami, "so I would like to ask you a medical question. What enables me to raise my hand?" As he said this he raised his hand. The doctor thought it was a silly question but answered: "You do so by a command of the conscious mind to which the nerves and muscles respond." "Can you do the same?" came the surprising challenge. "Of course," responded the doctor as he lifted his hand in imitation of the swami's gesture. "That is a simple action, and one which you can do without," remarked the swami. "But as you are speaking with me your heart is beating, your lungs are expanding and contracting, your blood pressure and body temperature are being maintained, and all the functions necessary to maintain life are going on completely without either your conscious thought or conscious volition. Tell me, Mr. Doctor: *Who* is doing that? You need to seek out the one who is maintaining your life in this way. This is your true Self, and without knowing it you are nothing but a puppet."

Now Dr. Mukherji was used to everyone treating him with respect and even deference because of his medical degree. As a consequence, he, too, had a rather good opinion of himself. But with these simple words the swami revealed the ignorant condition of all unenlightened human beings. Fortunately, in time (after three years!) Dr. Mukherji became a disciple of this monk, and came to discover the identity of the inner warrior.

The inner warrior is our true Self, our inner divinity which knows quite well why it has come into this world, and if not hindered by the lower self it will accomplish the purpose of its incarnation: our perfection and enlightenment. It is only this inmost part of ourselves that can win the battle of life. What, then, is to stand aside to let this warrior fight? It is the lower self, revolving around our false ego, that must be put to one side if the inner warrior is to manifest and triumph.

Lest we mistake the nature of the war, thinking that it is an external process, the Master says: "Let him fight *in* thee." All transformation, all true spiritual life, is an interior process, although it certainly is reflected in and even supported by external factors. But those who have nothing but external philosophizing and observance have not even entered the first gate of Wisdom (Jnana). The ego, being outside of us (that is, outside our true Self, the spirit), continually attempts to assert its dominance by luring us into externality and making us mistake it for spiritual realities. If it cannot succeed in this, it takes another tack and becomes extremely philosophical, attempting by a false non-dualism or an abstract "pure spirituality" to dissuade us from engaging in any outer disciplines which would facilitate our inner awakening.

The truth is, valid spiritual search involves a myriad of external actions and observances that are expressions of spiritual awakening as well as the means to increase that awakening. True spiritual life does not consist in mere abstraction but requires objectification of any inner unfoldment. Yet, the objectifications are but indications and symptoms of spiritual progress, and not the state of evolution itself. As with most things, the truth falls between the two extremes.

3. Take his orders for battle and obey them.

The real battle is within, yet as has been indicated above, it is also reflected outwardly. The lower self needing to be transmuted, it is necessary that it also engage in the struggle, but only as an instrument of the higher Self. So, although it seems contradictory, the battle must be fought both inwardly and outwardly, with the consciousness of the spirit as the one true doer.

Obviously we cannot take the orders of our higher self if we are not in touch with it and capable of perceiving its directives. Unless the various energies that make up our many bodies are purified to the utmost extent, it is impossible for genuine spiritual communication to take place. However, purification through diet, reformation of life, and purity of morals, though *essential*, are not in themselves sufficient. The ear of our purified energies must become attuned to the voice of the spirit. For this, the practice of meditation is indispensable.

Perhaps we should look at this expression: battle. Those who are "lovers not fighters" need not enlist in the ranks of the disciples of any religion, for all traditions indicate that the process of spiritual perfection is a great struggle to the death: the death of the ego and its attendant ignorance. Regarding the path of true perfection through inner and outer warfare, it can be said as truly as it was regarding the American westward expansion: "The weak died along the way, and the cowards never started." Those who do not wish to struggle unto death/life cannot but fail if they take up this path. Note that I speak of those who do not wish to do so, for in truth there are none who are incapable of success in spiritual life, although this is a popular excuse of the willfully lazy and ignorant. The simple fact of being a human being guarantees our ability to attain spiritual perfection if we will.

It is indeed true that merely being a human being does not enable us to engage successfully in this war, but it does mean that we can learn how to fight under the direction of the spirit-self and not under the lying usurper, the ego. Some people become disciples but follow the wrong commander. Letting themselves be attuned back to the ways of earth, they begin to heed the voice of the not-self and swear allegiance to it. And like the folly it is, it leads them into death rather than life.

Therefore the aspirant to discipleship should at the outset examine himself to see if he has the necessary disposition of will to accomplish his desire. He should know that the price is not paid in dribbles or installments, but that from the beginning he must lay all upon the line without reservation. Those who hope for a closeout sale, layaway plan or installment plan in spiritual life have simply not understood its and their nature. Nor should it be thought that the disciple can take time out in this battle to indulge the egoic desire for cessation of struggle. Just as the worthy soldier is a soldier every moment of his life and is at all times on call, so the disciple must always be in readiness for the battle. In fact, he should be perpetually engaged in the battle. Just as a soldier never forgets his vocation, neither can the disciple.

> Simple Simon met a pieman,
>   Going to the fair.
> Said Simple Simon to the pieman,
>   "Let me taste your ware."
>
> Said the pieman unto Simon,
>   "Show me first your penny."
> Said Simple Simon to the pieman,
>   "Indeed I have not any."

There are myriads of spiritual Simple Simons wandering about, but few are those who possess the penny to obtain the pie. So by employing this terminology the Master indicates the serious and total commitment necessary for spiritual attainment.

And obey them. It is easy to understand that if soldiers fought according to their own style whenever and wherever they felt it was "the right thing," there would not only be no victory, there would be their annihilation. It is essential that soldiers hear the orders and obey. There is no place in battle for argumentation, discussion or demands for justification of the orders. Fortunately, in spiritual life the disciple employs his intelligence, and in a viable spiritual system as much information as possible is imparted by the teacher. Yet, there are areas and periods of spiritual life in which the inexperienced disciple cannot intellectually comprehend the whys and wherefores of the fight. At this point the greatest amount of will power must be exerted. That is, the disciple does not surrender his intelligence and will and meekly acquiesce to incomprehensible orders, but rather with full determination he must move ahead without hesitation, and discover by himself the intention and meaning of the commands received. Because of this, throughout the lives of those who have attained the spiritual heights we find that they have had at times to do things which appeared to their inexperienced minds as utterly futile, absurd or even dangerous. Yet, having performed those required acts, they reaped great benefits. Let me give three examples known to me personally:

1) A man with severe gastro-intestinal illness appealed to an Indian saint for help. The saint's advice was that he eat in large quantities those items which his physician had told him would be fatal for him. He did so unhesitatingly, and was immediately and permanently cured.

2) An acquaintance of mine had lived in Warsaw, Poland. Being very poor, he and a friend frequently slipped into the estate of a wealthy man and caught fish. They knew that this was a most risky thing to do, because anyone caught would be given the severest sentence by the judges because of the rich man's political influence. The verdict of guilty and severe penalty was assured for anyone caught poaching. The two boys were caught, indicted, and a court date was set, though they

were allowed to go free in the meantime. Sure that they would be given a heavy jail sentence, especially because they were Jews, they appealed to a renowned Hasidic rabbi who told them to search through Warsaw and find the smallest padlock available. They followed this seemingly nonsensical directive and for two weeks spent their days and nights searching for the smallest padlock they could find. The rabbi told them that one of them should have this padlock in his pocket when they went into the courtroom. They did so, and the judge, a longstanding friend of the rich man who had often severely punished people to please him, threw the case out of court and severely rebuked the wealthy man to his face for treating the young men so harshly.

3) A monastic novice woke up one morning in terrible pain, hardly able to move. By forcing himself to move, he managed to get to the abbot's room, though once there he could not describe to him what he felt, because his teeth were literally chattering from the pain. Instead of showing sympathy, the abbot complained at him for wasting his time, and then in a disgusted though offhanded way commented that perhaps he just needed a drink of water! Although it was a tremendous struggle, the novice managed to get down the stairs and into the kitchen where he drank a glass of water. As the water drained down his throat, the pain drained completely away.

What was the secret of these three incidents? It was not obedience in the negative sense of canceling out one's intelligence and individual will. Rather, it was the exercise of will in the understanding that there are higher laws which operate within our lives. Also, the act of will linked the consciousness of the "obedient" to the enlightened will of the one giving the directions, and this alignment made healing and help possible.

For a person unacquainted with modern ways, the idea that light can be produced by the flipping of a switch is idiotic. To the inexperienced, the idea that the voice or image of a person on the other side of the world can be produced by turning a knob on a radio or television set seems equally mad. Those who first tried to fly failed because they quite logically imitated the only flying creatures they knew: birds. When a completely different process was employed using the principles of aerodynamics, human beings were able rise into the air and fly. It was senseless to think that several hundred people could fly in a steel contraption weighing many tons, but today they do. Human beings now accomplish numberless goals because they have discovered the laws for their accomplishment. But before the discovery of those laws, such accomplishments were considered "against nature." Thus, although many of the hidden laws of spiritual evolution are revealed to the disciple, the time does come (more than once) when the disciple must discover further laws on his own. And the gateway to those discoveries is the willful following of the prior commands.

Again let us look at the implications of "Take his orders for battle." As has already been stated, the aspirant must be ready for struggle and effort. There are those who expect that becoming disciples will put an end to all their troubles both internal and external. There is a great bid in the pseudo-spiritual world for "peace" of all kinds. But any true spiritual path involves internal warfare. Those who instead of a sword want the peace which one modern philosopher has described as "the feverlessness of a corpse" should not approach the fires of discipleship.

Further, since the warfare is internal so also must we understand the enemy to be internal. Looking within ourselves we find that we are morally divided. One part of us tends toward the light that is spirit, and one part of us tends toward the darkness that is our ego. As long as there is no sustained spiritual endeavor, the spiritual sleeper has no problem. He may simply attend one of the exoteric churches to pay his "dues" to God and go away having been entertained by the singing of the choir, challenged and uplifted by the words of the preacher and secure in the feeling of being part of a community. In other words, he can go away "feeling good" about himself and utterly satisfied. But those who would awake and arouse themselves for the journey into light experience something quite different, for immediately the resistance of their dark side comes into play and they have to confess with the cartoon character, Pogo: "We have met the enemy, and he is us!"

This is not pleasing to the ego and, having been assiduously avoided for ages, everything will be done to deny it. This is why the falsely "good" and the falsely "virtuous" avoid real spiritual life. Under the veil of noble philosophy and occasional good deeds, they conceal the enemy hidden within their own breast. But it cannot be so for the disciple. Rather, there must be a direct facing of all elements of darkness and ignorance that nest within our own hearts. And that darkness and ignorance must be dispelled. There are no cease-fires, no compromises, no peace treaties in the disciplic life. The enemy must be *destroyed*. Actually, that which momentarily appears as darkness is transmuted into light, but in the eyes of the ego, the master of that darkness, it appears to be destruction and death.

So right away the disciple must learn to do two contradictory things: squarely face his inner negativity and ruthlessly war with it, and at the same time keep his eyes on the perfection of God rather than his own imperfection. One ploy of the ego is to get the disciple to become discouraged over his inner evil, and to make him identify with it through shame. While the spectacle of our inner cesspool(s) is quite horrible, we must view the inner filth in the perspective of God's holiness: a holiness which is essentially ours and which we must consciously reclaim. We are indeed weak, and must have the good sense to realize it. Yet we must not identify with our weakness but with the conquering strength of God and our true spirit-Self.

We war against disease because we are aware of the possibility of health and have that goal in mind. Our real interest is not the disease or even the short-term goal of its annihilation, but rather the establishment of our health which is our natural and therefore rightful state.

This must be the perspective and attitude of the disciple. If we maintain this perspective, then the inner carnage, though not pleasant, will yet be neither discouraging nor overwhelming to us.

It should also be understood that the voice of the higher Self will speak to us only of the battle, and the same is true of those teachers illumined by their own higher Self. I mention this because there are those who want to get everything from spiritual life *except* spiritual life. They demand that their higher consciousness and external spiritual teachers give them the means to obtain their desires: all the way from personal health to political dominance. While the fraudulent ego and fraudulent teachers cheerfully comply with these demands (as they must, since they give no true spiritual enlightenment or directive), the higher Self and the saints of God do not. Nor will the higher Self and the saints assist us in roving pointlessly through the realms of the psychic. Those who seek lesser attainments than those of the spirit shall find their own higher Self and the saints of no avail.

Many years ago I met a woman who approached a highly developed yogi with a question. "I want to know just one thing," she told him. "Can you help me grow a new set of teeth?" When diplomatically told that this was not his specialty(!), she went away without a backward glance. Those who seek for spiritual life must determine that they will be satisfied with nothing else than life in the spirit. And they should expect to receive nothing else.

Face-to-face realization of Truth gives one intuitive conviction and true vision and understanding. Our seeking must be for the realm of spirit alone. If we truly have this as our only goal, then the supreme Spirit will itself supply everything that we need, but not a single unneeded thing that we may merely desire. Since we are dealing with Omniscience, it is impossible to deceive It into thinking that we are seeking for the highest alone when in reality we are only pretending to do so in the hopes that we shall get the promised "perks." Here, too, God is not mocked (Galatians 6:7), and we reap only what we actually sow. In Jane Eyre we read of a little boy who, when asked if he would rather learn a verse of the Psalms or be given a cookie, always said that he preferred the Psalm to the cookie, and as a consequence received two cookies. He was held up as a spiritual example by his foolish and vain father who did not realize that the boy had simply caught on to the strategy for getting cookies. Such things cannot take place in true spiritual life. We must decide what we want and go after it. And we must go after it in the right way and in the right place.

4. Obey him not as though he were a general, but as though he were thyself, and his spoken words were the utterance of thy secret desires; for he is thyself, yet infinitely wiser and stronger than thyself. Look for him, else in the fever and hurry of the fight thou mayest pass him; and he will not know thee unless thou knowest him. If thy cry meet his listening ear, then will he fight in thee and fill the dull void within. And if this is so, then canst thou go through the fight cool and unwearied, standing aside and letting him battle for thee. Then it will be impossible for thee to strike one blow amiss. But if thou look not for him, if thou pass him by, then there is no safeguard for thee. Thy brain will reel, thy heart grow uncertain, and in the dust of the battle filed thy sight and sense will fail, and thou wilt not know thy friends from thy enemies.

He is thyself, yet thou aft but finite and liable to error. He is eternal and is sure. he is eternal truth. When once he has entered thee and become thy warrior, he will never utterly desert thee, and at the day of the great peace he will become one with thee.

Obey him not as though he were a general, but as though he were thyself, and his spoken words were the utterance of thy secret desires; for he is thyself, yet infinitely wiser and stronger than thyself.

Why? Because he is not external to us, but is our own inmost Self. That, of course, is said later on in the sentence, but for now let us consider the implications of the opening phrase. It has already been pointed out that obedience is an act of will, yet the obedience which a soldier gives to a general may arise from factors completely undesirable in the spiritual aspirant. For one thing, the obedience may arise from ignorance, the assumption that the general knows what he does not know. Yet the soldier-disciple must be a man of knowledge. A soldier may also obey because he fears the punishment he would receive if he was slack or disobedient. The disciple must seek God because he values God above all else, not because he fears the censure or disapproval of God or any punishment from God.

A pause to look at the Bhagavad Gita on this subject will help us. There we are told: "Among the virtuous, four kinds seek me: the distressed, the seekers of knowledge, the seekers of wealth and the wise. Of them, the wise man, ever united, devoted to the One, is pre-eminent. Exceedingly dear am I to the man of wisdom, and he is dear to me. All these indeed are exalted, but I see the man of wisdom as my very Self. He, with mind steadfast, abides in me, the Supreme Goal. At the end of many births the wise man takes refuge in me. He knows: All is Vasudeva. How very rare is that great soul" (7:16-19). The search for God is the search for the Self.

This also brings to mind the fact that although it is a laudable thing to wish to flee sorrow and attain peace, if the basis of the disciple's search is simply the desire to avoid pain and attain happiness, he will inevitably fail, for his goal must be God, Who is beyond those dualities. The obedience of the soldier may also spring from the hope of recognition and personal reward. This attitude, too, is deadly for the disciple. Those who wish recognition in spiritual life are servants of the ego, not the spirit. Such persons disdain the humble and simple means which the sages have given us to scale the heights of the spirit.

The soldier may obey the commands of his general simply because everyone else is doing so. There are those who always want to know how many people adhere to a philosophy before they agree to adopt it. Such persons would never have joined themselves unto Christ and his impoverished little band. If they see that a multitude of people are following a path, then they are ready to fall in step, feeling secure in numbers. But with the disciple it is otherwise. Even though millions might be following the path of the disciple, each one will be following it alone: but alone with God. If God alone is not sufficient for us, then we have no business setting foot upon the highway of holiness. This is just good sense, as a little reflection can reveal. If this battle—and therefore this victory—is internal, then how could it involve anyone else but ourselves? Certainly the company of other true seekers is of great benefit and even a blessing, but often the disciple will know no one like himself. Those who "need" community and association with like-minded companions will not find the path of the disciple at all congenial. For one of the purposes of any legitimate spiritual system is the development to the fullest of the individual's capacities.

A soldier may obey simply because he thinks or has been told it is the right thing to do. Many people take up what they think is spiritual life because they have become convinced that it is the right or safe thing to do. This implies that they want to be thought the right sort by others and to receive the reward of "the righteous." Being egoic in nature, such motivation prevents the aspirant from entering upon the path of the spirit. As has been said, the soldier may not himself have decided to take up warfare, but rather has been urged to it by outside factors. Since the battle is internal, no external factors should (or even can) enter into this, for as has also been said, the battle is a solitary endeavor. Why then obey this general? Because he is *you.* We have come back full circle.

Look for him, else in the fever and hurry of the fight thou mayest pass him.

134

I think we have all seen this phenomenon. How many people have been so absorbed in "serving God" that they ignored God completely, their busywork "service" eliminating him from their lives. We especially see this in movements that have a "message." There are the movers and go-getters that are busily missionarying others. There are those brisk, efficient and vocal people who seem to be living for nothing but "the cause." Yet, when questioned closely, they will be discovered to have never studied their principles in depth and (if such is a part of the "message") neither do they engage in the practices which they so busily are cajoling others into. And "busy" is their watchword-rationalization. "Oh, I am just so busy promoting The Work that I have never had time to read that," or "No, I have just been so busy getting things organized and spreading The Word, that I never have time for meditation"–or whatever it is that they tell everybody else to do. These are truly the empty trash cans that rattle so aggressively. If we carefully observe missionaries of any sort we will discover that their missionarying is a cover for their own slackness, insecurity and emptiness. They are dedicated to harvesting, but not to the Lord of the Harvest; they are wells without water, clouds without rain.

So we must fight, but our eyes must not be on the fight but on the "general" of the fight: God the Self of our Self. Only those who keep their eyes continually fixed upon God can ever do the true, inner work of God and become one with God.

Let us not pass by two of the words in this phrase: fever and hurry. This is an assurance that the battle will indeed become heated and at times even hectic. Again, those who want the peace of inactivity will be disappointed in disciplic life. It is essential for the disciple to be always at fever-pitch and ready for more. I frequently liken the life of the disciple to jumping on the back of a tiger. The ride is terrifying, but the consequences of getting off are much worse, though many (if not most) do, and in consequence are eaten alive by the fangs and claws of ignorance.

And he will not know thee unless thou knowest him.

Obviously, the word "know" has a greater connotation than in its common usage. To be known by our own higher self, the individualized spirit, and the Supreme Self, God, is to have a dynamic communion established between us and those divine entities.

Not only are we mirrors of God, God is also a mirror of us. Therefore when we look to God he looks to us; when we hear God he hears us; when we call unto God he calls unto us; and when we strive to know him he knows us in the sense of acknowledgment and communication with us.

It is crucial that we understand the nature of the word "self." Many people think that self-knowledge consists in studying the psychology of their egoic mind. Some even think that self-knowledge is arrived at by studying their genealogy. But we must always distinguish between the lie and the truth–that is, between the ego-mind-body complex (including all the astral and causal bodies) and the pure consciousness which is not only our essential nature, but our *only* nature. We must come to the knowledge of ourselves as waves of light within the ocean of light that is God. And so, when we speak of Self-knowledge we are speaking exclusively of the knowledge of the eternal spirit, the true "us." If, however, we make the body and (lower) mind the basis, the frame of reference for the "fight," then truly all hell breaks loose, for the fight can only be waged in and by the spirit.

If thy cry meet his listening ear, then will he fight in thee and fill the dull void within.

We see the world filled with religion, but very little spiritual attainment. Why is this? The founders of all true religions spoke from the consciousness of pure spirit. Those who heard them, being enmeshed in the nets of both material and psychic existence and held under the hitherto undisputed sway of the ego, heard the words of the ever-free within the context of their bondage and quite naturally turned the words that were spirit and life into words of matter and mind. But if they caught the message of the necessity for transcendence of matter and mind, through following the teachings of the masters they transferred the focus of their consciousness into spirit and successfully liberated themselves from the ancient bondage. Functioning in their true nature as spirits, they attained true freedom: liberation.

"*If* thy cry…." Spiritual life depends upon the correctness of our approach to God. Just as there is a right and wrong way to use mechanisms of communication such as the telephone, so there are right and wrong ways to attempt communication with the Supreme Reality. The master wants the aspirant to understand this and therefore weigh carefully every aspect of his search to make sure that all is as it should be. Just as a sensible driver checks over his vehicle from time to time, and during his driving keeps an eye on the various indicators, so also must the spiritual aspirant do. I once heard a sermon entitled "Doing the Right Thing in the Right Way in the Right Place at the Right Time for the Right Reason." If we do not have all five of these Rights, then our spiritual endeavors will be either fruitless or produce a negative effect.

Again: "If thy *cry*…." The master uses the word "cry" to convey the necessity of total mind-gripping intensity of spiritual desire on our part. God does not hear the equivalent of a whisper, a mumble, a quiet speaking, or even an emphatic statement on our part. Rather, the spiritual equivalent of the "Man Overboard!" cry is needed for us to gain a response from God.

Sri Ma Anandamayi commonly addressed all men as "father." Once a man, sitting directly in front of her, asked: "Ma, why does God not answer our prayers?" Mother turned Her head to one side and absent-mindedly muttered "Father," in a low tone. Turning to the other side, She did the same, but slightly louder. Looking down at Her hands, Mother repeated "Father" in a conversational tone. Then, looking directly into his eyes,

She shouted "Father!" as She gestured toward him. Taken by surprise, he jumped to his feet, joined his hands in salutation, and responded: "Yes, Ma, what is it?" Mother began laughing merrily and replied: "I have given you your answer. You did not answer my saying 'Father,' until I directed my attention to you completely and called out with intense concentration. So it is with you and God. Change the way you pray, and you will get an answer."

Keeping in mind that the Master is speaking of both the individual Self and the cosmic Self, we must also realize that we cannot "get in touch with ourselves" without equal intensity on our part. Just as the scum floats on the surface of the water, veiling the water from our eyes, so the body, mind, and ego are blinding us to our true Self, stifling the Self and rendering it inoperative. Therefore intense and sustained effort is needed to remove the veils and let the Self shine forth. This is why in oriental philosophy it is often stated that the individual Self is very hard to find, but that once this is done, then God is relatively easy to find. First we must realize (awaken) our individual spirit before there is any possibility of our realization of the infinite Spirit. This is why the great Indian philosopher, Sri Ramanuja, taught that Self-realization was the prerequisite for God-realization.

We are told that God must hear, see, and know us. Since God is an omniscient being, how is it possible for anything to be unheard, unseen, or unknown by Him? Obviously this is impossible. But the inspired writers are thinking in a totally pragmatic or practical sense. Although God does indeed hear, see and know us in the highest levels of being, it is meaningless unless it is translated into direct operation within our lives. That is, God must become operative within the spheres of our interior and external existence. Otherwise, for all practical purposes God does not even exist–at least for us.

We, on the other hand, having awakened after the course of countless ages of virtual spiritual unconsciousness, need to arouse our true selves.

138

Then we will find that God, too, will awake and arise in relation to us. We have to face the fact that throughout the ages which have lapsed during our numberless incarnations, the debris of ignorance has steadily accumulated, suffocating us and cutting us off from all sight and communication with God. We must eliminate one by one the obstacles we have placed between us and God until the effects of our karmic "sowing" throughout previous births have been undone.

To enter upon the path of discipleship is to begin the Great Work of spiritual alchemy, the transmutation of the presently human into the divine. In other words, it is the Great Struggle. And it is death we are talking about: the death of our lower nature and all ties to the world's lower evolution; death that must be voluntarily undergone in order that we may rise into true life, the life of the living spirit. These are not very inspiring, or perhaps even motivating, words, but they are necessary for the serious seeker to face. Before we begin our spiritual endeavor we must calmly, honestly and intelligently consider what is required of us to succeed. Then we will be prepared for any difficulties along the way.

Part of the necessary process is the expunging of all the negative and delusive conditionings produced in us by countless earthly incarnations, conditionings which are present within us at this moment as vital factors within the hidden depths of our mind which itself has become corrupted into our enemy.

We have been conditioned to externality and materiality through our experience in the many bodies which we have inhabited during our incarnations. Because of this conditioning, all of our bodies, gross and subtle, including the desire and will bodies, are polarized to material consciousness. As a result, we have for incarnation after incarnation refused to even listen to the truths of higher consciousness. Then for more lives we listened, but only passively, and did not do a single thing about it. Now, in this incarnation, we have decided to stand up, equip ourselves and take the long, blessed journey of return to our original home in God.

But this decision is often both nebulous and tenuous. We neither know what our rising and going will entail, nor do we really will it except with the minutest portion of our intellect. Everything else that is "us" is against us in this matter. Yet, all the elements of our being must in time be polarized to this holy intention and turned into instruments for its accomplishment. For this to occur, we must grapple with them one by one and submit them to our will. Our many levels (bodies) are not of themselves evil, but they have been negatively polarized and turned away from the truth we seek to unveil. We may think of our many bodies and faculties as the flock of a shepherd which have strayed and become wild. Before they can be returned to the fold where they belong, they will have to be both captured and tamed. Although I have used the simile of sheep, most of them are more like wild horses and wild elephants than merely skittish sheep. Consequently, spiritual life is much more like bronco busting than the effortless ethereal fantasy most of us hold. We like to think of ourselves as floating angels rather than sweating wranglers, but that is exactly what we must become, at least in the spirit.

Spiritual life cannot be encompassed by the superficial desire of the mind. Those who attempt spiritual life with such a basis will ultimately give up in frustration. To bring together all the components of our being and harmonize them with divine consciousness is as futile for the mind as the counting of the grains of sand on the ocean floor. It is just simply beyond the mind's scope. Anyone who has ever tried the path of "positive thinking" or "replacing bad habits with good habits" knows how in time those endeavors prove to be utterly worthless. What then is to be done? Exactly what the Master tells us: we must rouse up the divine in us, for only the spirit, being the source of all, is capable of gathering all the aspects of our being into one and directing them toward the divine goal. For this reason, mere mind games, however noble and philosophical they might seem, are futile. Rather, we must go directly to the spirit. Even more, we must *activate* the spirit. Spiritual consciousness has been symbolized throughout the ages by the rising sun. Much of the physical world lies dormant and silent in the night, but at dawn everything comes to life around us, as we have all experienced.

Again, we must realize that the Master is telling us to tap into our inmost consciousness which is the spirit. This is done primarily through the practice of meditation in which we contact the transcendent aspect of our being. This divine entity, our spirit, is the source of all the external levels of our being. Just as God the infinite emanates all the evolutionary worlds we call "creation," so in the same way our individual spirit, god the finite, has emanated the multifarious bodies in which we find ourselves. Therefore it alone can really encompass and master them and transmute them back into pure spirit, thus completing its own evolution.

It is crucial for spiritual aspirants to realize that the path to God must begin with God. Right away we must be contacting God and invoking the divine consciousness within. This sounds like an extremely difficult thing to accomplish, and if the aspiration was all on our part alone, it would be not only be difficult, it would be impossible. But the Master has told us a wonderful fact when he says: "If thy cry meet his listening ear…." By this he indicates that God the Infinite and god the finite (our own spirit) is ever listening for our call. God is not far away, nor is he asleep or deaf. Rather, he is nearer than our own thoughts and is conscious of every movement within our being. It is we who are failing to get the message, not God, and we must realize that.

At the same time we can be one hundred percent optimistic about God's attention to us. To speak of God's "listening ear" is to also indicate that God is ready to hear our call and to respond. Although everything is just fine on God's end, things are clogged up on our side, and that is why the Master has put the word "if" in his statement. But this need not worry us, for when we apply the spiritual methodology of yoga, it is not our lesser power or lesser will that is involved, but rather the divine power and will of our own divine spirit and ultimately—since our spirit is rooted in God and takes its very existence from him—the infinite power and will of God.

However restless and distracted the mind may be at times in meditation and throughout the day, it is still in the midst of the divine world through its invocation of the divine consciousness through japa of the mantra Soham as outlined in *Soham Yoga: The Yoga of the Self.* Again, we can be thoroughly optimistic regarding the eventual outcome of our meditation and invocation if they are steadily maintained, for it is the divine power which is acting in us through such activity. The divine seed, when carefully tended, will in time come to full growth and fruition. Patience is needed to persevere in our spiritual endeavors and in our waiting for the results of those endeavors. In time we shall master the totality of our existence. However, that will not be the end but only the beginning. We must then begin the return of ourselves to pure spirit which is consciousness.

When our cry does in truth reach the listening ear of the divine Self, the principle of pure evolution, the force that impels us to return to God, arises and makes war with the ancient power of delusion and ignorance that has gripped us throughout creation cycle after creation cycle, even ascending into the "heaven" of our consciousness and darkening it to the point of seeming extinguishment, and in this way plunging us into total material awareness, at least on the conscious "waking" level of the mind.

It is the spirit alone that wages the divine warfare, for it is the spirit alone that can win. Those whose minds, emotions, and intellects direct the warfare are doomed to defeat, by the very nature of their "warriors." Thus if we would be successful in spiritual life we must see that it is indeed that: *spiritual.* And meditation is the means of ensuring that our warfare is spiritual. Such a warfare is, as we say, invincible and shall lead in time to victory unless, tragically lead astray by Satan (the power of delusion in the cosmos and our energy makeup), we cry "halt" to the endeavor. And this does, indeed, happen.

From the Master's words we can infer that one sign of being truly spiritually awakened is the process of inner warfare. Many, possessing an utterly false understanding of religious and spiritual life, engage in external warfare, enmeshed in their egoic minds and their concerns with the external world and its inhabitants. This futile warfare takes a myriad of forms, all the way from substituting good thoughts for bad thoughts and "cleaning up the vocabulary" to the writing of hysterical polemics against "heresies" and even the ultimate folly of imprisoning or killing "heretics." We, too, must be vigilant in our spiritual life, and make sure that we do not slip into a like error. For although spiritual life must of necessity be manifested externally, it nevertheless is ever based in the spirit and is at all times directed by the spirit. We often begin with warfare in the spirit but our habit of ego-dominance draws us away into the warfare centered in lesser realms.

It should be realized, then, that the truly spiritually awakened are not those that smile with wan sweetness and speak of their "great peace" or their supposed illumination. Rather, they are those who make no claims whatsoever about their spiritual life because they are much too busy successfully leading it. Those spiritual teachers or teachings that do not make the necessity for interior warfare clear to us are not worthy of our attention.

Just how will our spirit carry on the interior warfare? This is an important question, as millions of deluded people throughout the world are convinced that God is talking to them or managing their lives or that their higher selves are in control when in actuality their satanic ego is in total domination. The truth is that our spirit wages war with but one weapon: the invocation of higher consciousness through meditation and japa. This is literally so, and not to be taken symbolically. Our spiritual will is the sword in the hand which casts out Satan from us. Ultimately everything that exists is one with God. However, all objects within creation appear to have an existence independent of God, and are actually veils which hinder our seeing the truth of their essential being: God.

Authentic spiritual life, especially in the beginning, is often more frightening than it is reassuring. There is a rather daunting picture of the account of the defeat of the evil forces by the Mother aspect of God that is found in the Hindu scripture known as the Chandi or Sri Devi Mahatmyam. There the Mother roves over a great battlefield, cutting off the heads of demons with her sword. This is a symbolic portrayal of the descent of the illumining power of God and its destruction of evil. This is the only possible spiritual victory.

How do we attain peace? By transferring the center of our consciousness from the never-peaceable world to the ever-peaceable spirit. Peace is not a state of mind or emotion, for the mind and emotions are by their nature in constant flux and incapable of peace, but is rather the permanent condition of the spirit. The wise know that there can never be peace on earth, but there is ever peace in the spirit. However, everything comes with a price, and the price of true interior peace is interior war.

The advent of the divine consciousness into that of the devoted disciple produces an impartial and shadowless light of inner perception by means of which the disciple sees fully all that is within him and discerns truly its character. This is not a particularly enjoyable experience since, except for our pure spirit, all that is within us is darkened and defiled with ignorance and delusion. If the light that produces this revelation was merely of our own intellect, we would understandably become depressed and discouraged. But since it is the light of our true Self that shines, we are actually made optimistic, even cheerful, by it, for that light reveals to us that all darkness and delusion is merely temporary, only an illusion that shall be dispelled in time through our perseverance in spiritual endeavor. "You have to be cruel to be kind," certainly applies to the advent of inner Light into our life. To our ego the resulting illumination will appear merciless to the ego—and so it is. But to the imprisoned spirit it is the sweet dew of mercy, for it will not allow a single bond to remain upon it.

Those who have experienced that light must straightaway set about scrutinizing every aspect of their existence, internal and external. And this must be done without sparing the egoic likes and dislikes of either ourselves or others. It is essential that we force ourselves to face the total truth about ourselves and that with which we have mistakenly identified through so many incarnations.

A typical person, including a typical spiritual seeker, is usually completely unaware of his inner, or subconscious, mind. Everything seems to be just fine, and he is confident that he is indeed a temple of God, that in him dwells the eternal Spirit. And this is true, but there is more he needs to know. Being unaware of his inner mind, he perceives only the minor symptoms of its condition in the form of his conscious thoughts and impulses. Although they may not be completely positive, they do not seem to be very serious; in fact he usually looks upon them as harmless flaws which he hopes one day to correct. They appear to be of little significance. But these little flaws, when investigated, are seen to be of an entirely different character. They are not the little holes or cracks in the wall of consciousness which he thought they were, but they are actually immense doors: doors through which negative elements have entered into his being and festered there, poisonous and deadly.

"And he [a divine messenger] brought me to the door of the court; and when I looked, behold a hole in the wall. Then said he unto me, Son of man, dig now in the wall: and when I had digged in the wall, behold a door. And he said unto me, Go in, and behold the wicked abominations that they do here. So I went in and saw; and behold every form of creeping things, and abominable beasts, and all the idols of the house of Israel, pourtrayed upon the wall round about. And there stood before them seventy men of the ancients of the house of Israel, and in the midst of them stood Jaazaniah the son of Shaphan, with every man his censer in his hand; and a thick cloud of incense went up. Then said he unto me, Son of man, hast thou seen what the ancients of the house of Israel do in the dark, every man in the chambers of his imagery?" (Ezekiel 8:7-12).

Medical research has shown that the human body is teeming with parasites, bacteria, and viruses—all invaders alien and destructive to the body. So it is with us psychologically. When we begin to examine the wall of our mind which is separating us from higher consciousness, we will find that what at first appear to be small cracks or holes will with scrutiny be revealed as vast fissures and breaches which both weaken the structure and permit the influx of inimical elements. In other words, where before we perceived soundness we perceive decay and destruction. Through continual birth and death in the distorted realms of material existence, our entire inner makeup has likewise become distorted and turned into an instrument of spiritual blindness and bondage. This must be clearly perceived and remedied before there is any possibility of our moving along the upward path of spiritual evolution.

There is a story in India about some people who wanted to attend a wedding quite a distance from their home. In those days there were few roads, so rivers were used for travel. Since the journey would be long and the weather was hot, they decided to start out after dark and row all night so they would reach their destination before noon the next day. Getting into the boat they rowed all night, taking turns at the oars. When the sun rose they found to their chagrin that they had not moved one foot. Why? Because they had forgotten to pull in the boat's anchor. In the same way no spiritual efforts will avail if we are still tied to material consciousness by our acts and will.

Before we can even hope to impel the boat of our individual consciousness across the ocean of delusion to the shore of enlightenment, we must first detach ourselves from all things that keep us anchored in our present status. And we must not content ourselves with detachment from just one anchor, for we have numberless anchors holding us firmly to the shore of ignorance.

The bonds must be cut! Not just one bond or nearly all bonds, but every single one. And then we will find that we must teach ourselves to walk before we can escape our imprisonment. Furthermore, like the long-caged bird we will no doubt find the prospect of freedom terrifying and will have to force ourselves to escape the dungeon. Although the inner call to freedom may inspire us to some degree, we must get busy and begin loosening the bonds of personal ignorance and limitation until at last we are set free: both by God and by ourselves. The call to freedom is not enough; we need to tread the Way of Freedom as well.

Without clear and accurate interior judgement this is impossible. What is clear and accurate judgement? It is judgement according to the standards of the spirit, of the eternal verities. None of the delusive taint of relative finite existence is in the true judgment of spirit. Rather, everything is measured "with eternity's values in view," as a twentieth-century hymn says. We, therefore, must be sure that in all things our consciousness is attuned with the divine consciousness, and that we evaluate all things according to the ultimate values of the spirit.

It is obvious, then, that there can be no version of "situation ethics" or "non-judgmentalism" in the life of the spiritual aspirant. Absolutes are necessary; but they must be the divine absolutes and not those of our own limited thinking. This is why the saints and masters are always seen to be a (seeming) mixture of liberal and conservative attitudes, displaying both flexibility and inflexibility in their words and deeds. They simply operate according to a totally different system than that of the world. "The recollected mind is awake in the knowledge of the Atman which is dark night to the ignorant: the ignorant are awake in their sense-life which they think is daylight: to the seer it is darkness" (Bhagavad Gita 2:69). For the spirit alone is real, and therefore alone is true and right.

147

And only those who are centered in the right perspective of their own divine spirit can possibly judge accurately. But judge they must.

We have pretty well covered the idea that spiritual life must be a warfare, so we need not go into that at this point. However, we should note that the divine war comes as a natural consequence of the aspirant's right judgment. That is, having diagnosed the situation correctly, he responds in the correct mode, that of spiritual warfare, which is ultimately a matter of purification. Our divine selfhood is already a settled fact. It need not be attained, but rather revealed. The process of that revelation is the process of purification. So when we speak of warfare, we are not speaking of anger, hatred, or hostility, but of a *catharsis*, a thorough cleansing and purification such as gold undergoes in the fire when it is refined.

A more inward aspect of this subject is this: When the higher consciousness dawns within us, divine sight awakens and in some measure we come to see as God sees. Now that sounds very exalted, but what it really means is that his divine eye reveals to us all that lies within between us and our true spirit. In other words, the muck and debris of millions (if not billions) of incarnations is revealed in perfect and devastating clarity. This is because the ignorance must be cleared out of us before the truth of ourselves, of our spiritual being, can be discovered. Most people expect that when they sit to meditate they will be wafted away on a magic carpet of beatitude into the realms of infinite bliss. This is like a kindergartner expecting that on the first day of school he will receive his doctorate amidst gratifying applause. It will not happen!

"And I saw the dead, small and great, stand before God; and the books were opened: and another book was opened, which is the book of life: and the dead were judged out of those things which were written in the books, according to their works. And the sea gave up the dead which were in it; and death and hell delivered up the dead which were in them: and they were judged every man according to their works. And death and hell were cast into the lake of fire. This is the second death. And whosoever was not found written in the book of life was cast into the lake of fire" (Revelation 20:12-15).

I once heard a yogi say that meditation was the true confession, for the conscious and subconscious minds divulge all their secrets, most of them ugly as well as trivial. Rather than being a little event, this is usually a cataclysmic psychological process, part of the purification which is necessary for enlightenment. In meditation we are mistaken to be annoyed by the thoughts, memories, emotions, and other flotsam and jetsam which come floating into the focus of our consciousness. These are certainly objectionable if they manage to pull our mind away from the focus of meditation, yet we must understand that the meditation has itself evoked the rise of these negative elements so we can perceive and eliminate them through the very thing that revealed them: meditation. The light of the Self shines into the darkness of our ignorance and summons forth all that dwell therein. They stand before our awareness, their nature is clearly revealed, and they are dismissed: either to become a permanent part of our spiritual makeup or to be reduced to their basic constituent of primal consciousness and absorbed into the subtle power levels of our being, particularly that of the will. In other words, our inner citizens shall either be made immortal or dissolved through transmutation. The experiencing of this is not thrilling or something to write books about. Rather, it is tedious, disgusting, annoying, and even (if we permit it) discouraging.

It is not uncommon for meditators to complain about negative traits arising in their mind which they believed were already eliminated. It should be understood that the meditator is like a geologist boring through strata laid down through countless incarnations. Let us say we have been greedy to an extreme degree in a dozen past lives: not continuously, but with other lives in between in which we were not greedy. We may be forced to face the greed demon for quite a few meditations to eliminate it from the impressions produced in our most recent life. We may then spend weeks, months, or even years, moving through the debris of prior lives, only to one day find the greed imp facing us again, just as before. Although it is the same negative trait arising, it is in one sense not the same. That is, it is the greed germ of a life farther back. It will in time disappear, and then once more reappear when we get into the layer of another past life in which we were obsessively greedy. It is good to know this, so we will not mistakenly think that we are simply cycling the same negative impulses over and over, and not really getting anywhere. We are actually making great progress when this occurs. As can be imagined, this process may take a long time to get through. It is possible to clear the debris out in one lifetime, but diligent application is needed.

The most important thing in all of this, is to realize that successful meditation involves the seeming resuscitation of long-dead thoughts, desires, and habits of previous lives. Although meditation is the divine eye through which we perceive these ghosts, we are not to voluntarily seek for them nor are we to fix our attention on them and analyze them. Instead, we are to ignore them and keep on with the process of meditation. In this way we will directly experience what Saint Paul meant in saying that some men's sins go to judgement before them, and some men's sins follow after them (I Timothy 5:24). Those who practice the interior life find their sins judged and dealt with before the great summing up that takes place at physical death. Those who have no effective interior life will find their sins (negative karmas) coming after them and catching up with them at the great summation, and thereby impelling them into further earthly births.

It is possible to dissolve or clear out karma through meditation. The impressions which arise during meditation are not just simple memories or interior impressions; rather they are the karmic seeds from which the external factors we usually call "my karma" proceed. If these seeds are cauterized in meditation through the purifying vibrations of higher consciousness, they will not manifest in the future. In this way meditation becomes the fulfillment of the ancient counsel: "See that your past does not become your future." Meditation has the power to mitigate (lessen) our karma. If our karma is to break our leg, we may only suffer a painful blow to the leg instead.

Meditation also speeds up our karma. Therefore the disciple is seen to reap far more karma in a single lifetime than the non-disciple. Further, the initiate's karma is intensified: a karmic period that would ordinarily last several months or a year may last only a few weeks or days of great intensity. This is because the disciple can cope with karmic forces that would utterly overwhelm the non-disciple. Although, as has been said, meditation is healing, it has been my experience that the symptoms of an illness can be greatly magnified through meditation, thus making the illness of a much shorter duration. On the other hand, I have also found that meditation can greatly alleviate physical pain and lessen the discomfort of illness. All is done according to the infinite wisdom. One thing is sure: The current of meditation unerringly bears us to our true home in the heart of God.

If there is no war there cannot possibly be a victory. The great epic of India, the Mahabharata, is a masterful picture of the present condition of ignorant humanity. Because of their own folly, the legitimate rulers of the Pandava kingdom were forced to hand over the governance of the land to the evil Kauravas for a certain period of time, after which they were to reassume their administrative control. But when the time lapsed, the Kauravas refused to relinquish their power. So war was inevitable: a war in which, although the Pandavas were victorious, nearly all the warrior-ruler caste of India was destroyed.

So it is with us: we have foolishly relinquished the "kingdom" of our various bodies, including the mind and intellect, into the control of negativity and folly. Now we want this control back, but the mere wanting accomplishes nothing. We are going to have to fight; and in that battle most will not be merely bruised, but hacked to pieces. Spiritual life is for the slaying of evil as much as it is for the healing and restoration of the good. The inner Christ which we seek is not a little baby cooing in the manger. Rather, he is the fully-realized adult who drives from the temple of God all that defiles or is alien to it.

The battle for liberation of the spirit is not fought solely by the spirit against a virtually limitless number of foes in the form of karmas and samskaras, both negative and positive, as well the outer influences that go to make up the world of man and nature. It is our divine Self united with God who wages the battle of real spiritual struggle, so success is assured. On the other hand, the battles instituted by ego must by their very nature fail.

When the consciousness of our spirit begins to arise in the mind it is accompanied by all the powers inherent in us, powers which are also impulses toward the divine, rays of light emanating from our inmost being which is an image of the sun of divinity. It is these powers that annihilate all opposition however terrifying or mighty it might appear to be. For that appearance is a lie. We, our true Self and God, are the only Truth.

These divine powers must never be confused with the "natural" powers of corrupted human nature. All "good" wrought by such is either seen in time to be no good at all or to be ineffectual and ephemeral in nature. This is why so many seem to progress and then regress, to rise high and fall low. The seeming progress and ascent were effects of natural powers which ultimately could not avail. Without the power of spirit nothing of any real, lasting character can be accomplished. This is why, for example, religions of true wisdom never try to convert through enticement or persuasion. They know that any adoption of religious thought or action that does not spring from the awakening of the inmost consciousness of the pure Self or spirit can only go awry or collapse. Most religion at the present time is the expression of pathological conditions of body, mind, and emotion. This is the virulent fruit of missionarying.

In the matter of interior life it is particularly essential that all endeavor is motivated from the inmost consciousness of the seeker. Otherwise failure and harm (in the form of spiritual pain and damage) are the inevitable result. For this reason aspirants should scrupulously examine the nature of their spiritual interest and see it for what it truly is. So also must a legitimate teacher and guide determine the source of the inquirer's pursuit, and refuse to accommodate egoism or whimsey in any degree. The "will remodel to suit tenant" attitude of many teachers reveals their own incompetence and dishonesty.

How, then, can we ensure that it is the divine powers which are being evoked in us and not the ephemeral shades of ego? By the nature of our practice itself. It must be based from beginning to end on the invocation of the Divine Consciousness, the only commander around which the divine forces rally to do battle under its aegis. As already stated, this is the guarantor of success. And *Soham Yoga: The Yoga of the Self* gives the complete picture. (As do *Light of Soham* and *The Inspired Wisdom of Sri Gajanana Maharaj* as well.)

The inner spiritual powers are subtle, refined and light. So also are their effects. These powers are not cataclysmic in nature, producing extreme, violent or even readily perceived changes or effects. This is important to know, because presently it is considered desirable that spiritual practice should result in shakes, quakes, thrills, chills, sights, lights and other such gross phenomena that read well in a "how I got enlightened" book for popular consumption. But as Yogananda often reminded his students, "the path to the Divine is not a circus." In truth such phenomena as those just described are fundamentally pathological in nature, and those who undergo them are ultimately seen to be worsened rather than bettered, all effusive testimonial and insistence to the contrary. Here are two examples from life, both connected with each other.

One of Yogananda's disciples, Brahmacharini Forest, told me that she and many others were puzzled at the great difference they experienced when blessed by Yogananda and his most advanced male disciple, James Lynn (Rajasi Janakananda). "When Rajasi blessed us, it nearly blew the tops of our heads off," she said. "Sometimes people almost fell over backwards. But when Master blessed us we did not feel anything at all." This was often discussed by the various disciples, but they could not arrive at any conclusion. So Forest went to Sister Meera, one of the senior monastics, and asked her about the matter. "Sister Meera explained to me that Rajasi had a great deal of power, but did not know how to direct it. So he just threw it at us and literally bowled us over. Master, on the other hand, had perfect control, and when he blessed us he directed the currents deep into our physical and astral bodies, cleansing us from karmas and our negative subconscious habit patterns. We did not feel anything, because everything moved in the astral channels as they should without any resistance, and we were benefited by it."

This was my experience in relation to two of Yogananda's advanced disciples. When one touched me on the forehead I would feel tremendous spiritual force entering the "third eye" and flowing through the brain and spine. It was not violent, but it was very dramatic. In contrast, when the other disciple touched me in blessing I would feel nothing whatsoever. But in a few minutes, as I sat quietly, I would experience an indescribable elevation of consciousness and a deep, lasting inner awakening. It was when I referred to this in a conversation with Brahmacharini Forest that she told me her experience and Sister Meera's clarification.

It is the refined, subtle energies that are able to work lasting changes in our awareness. The more evolved consciousness or energy becomes, the more refined and subtle it becomes. Thus it is the highest level of spiritual powers alone that are able to conquer all opposition to our ascent to perfection. It is not the obvious energies of the objective levels of our being, including emotion or intellect, that can aid us in the struggle, for they are of mixed character: partly polarized to the lower, downward-pulling orientation of matter, and partly polarized to the higher, upward-tending pull of the spirit. By their very nature they create conflict in us, which is why responsible spiritual teachers emphasize the need for continual purification of the aspirant on all levels. For if the aspirant does not rise above these lower levels his spiritual life will continually swing like a pendulum between the opposites of higher and lower, outward and inner, consciousness. Many of my yogi friends experienced this because they did not work on purifying and refining the inner mechanism (antakarana). It was not their fault, because no one ever told them either the need for it or the way to do it. So they became spiritually manic-depressive.

One of my best friends was a yogi who lived just down the hall from my apartment. When I would knock on her door she would either open it right away with a cheerful smile or I would have to wait for a while, the door would swing open and I would go in and find her standing behind the door in tears. She was intelligent and devoted, a most worthy person, but because she was insufficiently instructed and guided (read: *completely* uninstructed and unguided) she continually flew high or crashed low. And, frankly, the very nature of the yoga she practiced did this to her.

The seeker must disentangle himself from such constant cycling, otherwise his life will be a frustrating series of ups and down, risings and fallings like the ever-moving waters of the ocean. For this reason we must continually strive to purify and refine our entire makeup, outer and inner, to ensure our success and stability in spiritual life. For this reason I strongly recommend that you read "The Foundations of Yoga," the sixth chapter of *Soham Yoga: The Yoga of the Self.*

Only the purified and refined aspirant can succeed, and his spiritual practice must correspondingly be of the highest character–not just the obvious and outer ways of exoteric religion, though they, too, are needed to maintain his pursuit. It is the subtle interior practices of yoga and meditation that must become the foundation of his spiritual attainment. The powers released by them are innate in each one of us, but are only activated through applications of the principles of yoga, both meditation and the requisite disciplines. It is these interior powers that grant victory to the aspiring soul, and upon which he continually draws. Here, too, the aspirant and his spiritual practice must be of the same nature.

It is spirit power that accomplishes our metamorphosis from the unreal to the Real, from darkness to the Light, from death to Immortality. Only the spirit truly aspires to Spirit. And the means of metamorphosis, the methods of inner alchemy, must be exclusively spiritual in nature. This is particularly crucial for the spiritual pilgrim, since most "spiritual practices" including most supposed yogic methods, are really physical, psychic or intellectual in nature and, like their impulses, can only lead back to them, however flashy or impressive they may be. In the end their practicers find themselves right where they started, however entertaining the experiences produced by them. Beginning in delusion, limitation and bondage, they end there, for actually they never really "took" the practicers anywhere. Years, lifetimes even, are frittered away by such methods that are very much like the revolving mirrored spheres seen on dance floors. They have no light of their own, distort what they reflect, and ultimately go dark.

A practice is spiritual and not illusive if it begins and ends in *consciousness*, and consciousness alone. That is, if its ultimate result is establishment in the pure consciousness that alone is the nature of our spirit–and of God. Such a practice is extremely hard to find, but not impossible. We must not unquestioningly accept the claims of a practice's promoters, but be very wary.

No one likes war, inner or outer, but for the aspirant to higher consciousness it is an absolute necessity. Without the struggle into the light, the seed will die; without the struggle to break open the egg and emerge, the chick will die; without the trauma of birth the infant in the womb will die. We fear a fight lest we be injured or killed, but unless we engage in the inner war, pain and death are inevitable. As in all other aspects, our outer life often renders us unfit for the inner life, since we assume the same rules apply and the experiences will be the same. But without the inner fight there is no inner fulfillment. The Master wants us to understand this well.

Aeons ago the spirit left its home in God and entered into the alien realm of relative existence. In that barren place it lost all knowledge of itself and God. By continual rebirth it became dominated by the senses. It yearns to satisfy itself with sensory experience, but being material, these experiences cannot touch, much less satisfy, the questing spirit. But they can delude it! And so the wandering soul drifts on, impelled by "the dull void within" and always in the wrong direction.

Educated in the school of this world, we fear pain. The struggle to avoid want and suffering is considered "the pursuit of happiness." And it is that struggle which robs us of "life" and "liberty" as well. How alienated we find ourselves from those "inalienable rights"! We plod on, absorbed in the ache of that "dull void within." Zombielike, we feed the senses and starve our souls, living the common life of "quiet desperation." But when we turn back into ourselves and send out the inner call, the divine spark fanned by our earnest cry bursts into living fire, fights and thereby fills that void with the inner light of the Self. Nothing else can fill that void and bring peace to the spirit. As John Oxenham wrote:

To every man there openeth
A Way, and Ways, and a Way,
And the High Soul climbs the High Way,

And the Low Soul gropes the Low,
And in between, on the misty flats,
The rest drift to and fro.
But to every man there openeth
A High Way, and a Low.
And every man decideth
The way his soul shall go.

The expression "dull void" conveys to us the truth about this world and its life: dreariness is its primary character. However raucous and gaudy, however frantic and explosive it may be, "after the ball is over" and the silence of the devastated heart alone remains, only weariness and hopelessness reigns. Dull of eye and soul we sink to earth and wallow in momentary oblivion, only to awaken to the whips and shouts of "the good life," struggle up and again stagger on in "the pursuit of happiness," leaving any hope of real life and liberty behind us undetected. How worn out we are. "The dullness of the tea-time of life" persists. Rare are those who rally enough to grieve with T. S. Eliot's J. Alfred Prufrock that "I have measured out my life in coffee spoons."

Rare are those who get even half of what the world and the ego promise.

This dull aching void is within, not without, and it is a grave error to suppose that any outer thing whatsoever can remove it. Those who frantically pursue pleasure or fulfillment outside themselves only compound their misery, even if momentarily they seem to gain what they desire. From life to life we assume that the void is outside us and seek to fill it by obtaining a myriad "things," only to be disappointed and impelled to run after the next object we mistakenly believe will satisfy us and remove our discontent.

It is especially crucial that we do not fall into the supposition that our problem is not an inner void, but some kind of inner state or entity that only needs to be changed or soothed: that nothing more is needed than the removal or anesthetizing of the pain. But our problem is an *absence*, a lack, a painful emptiness rather than just an undesired or undesirable presence or condition which is really only a symptom of the problem. Therefore it must be filled.

Unfortunately, although we cannot fill that inner void with outward things, we attempt to cram into our hearts all sorts of distractions and mental toys, not to speak of outright self-deceptions, and even illusions imposed upon us by others. Never do these things really fill us or dispel the sense of lack and emptiness, but we make ourselves think that, like medicine, they only need some time to work their cure. That, too, never occurs, and we keep running in the inner maze, grasping at anything in our mental reach and attempting to plug up the inner vacuum that gnaws at us perpetually. Only the spirit by its advent can work the cure and truly fill the dull void within.

Many fantasy or fairy stories from ancient times are really spiritual parables. Originally they were part of the inner tradition of the religions that were displaced by Christianity. Their theology was forgotten but the stories, since they drew upon subconscious roots that are common to all, remained fascinating to all generations. Sleeping Beauty is one such sacred myth. The spirit, asleep under the evil spell of ignorance, lies within the castle of the body as if dead. Impenetrable brambles encircle the castle, squeezing it like a malevolent serpent. Such are the negative forces we call karma that spring from our actions of past and present. Only through spiritual battle can the evil guardian of evil be slain, the brambles cut through and the princess be awakened to life. Tremendous is the war that the divine warrior must fight to enter the dull void of our heart and fill it with his Light. We must acknowledge this and prepare ourselves accordingly.

And if this is so, then canst thou go through the fight cool and unwearied....

159

Yes, there will be a fight. But we shall even then be at peace if we let the warrior work his will in us.

A devotee of Sri Ramakrishna told him of having a dream in which he saw a man walking easily and rapidly across the water of a vast sea. "How are you able to do that?" he called from the shore. Not looking back, the man replied: "It is easy. There is a bridge just beneath the surface of the water." "Wait for me, then," the dreamer called out. "No; I cannot wait. You come along in your own time," answered the man as he kept on walking. When Sri Ramakrishna heard this, He was profoundly thrilled and urged the man to take up spiritual practice immediately.

We think that leading a spiritual life of sufficient intensity to make a difference will be difficult and even painful. But we are wrong. Our problem is that we have a wrong understanding of just about everything to do with the higher life, and naturally it becomes a struggle and a frustration for us. But once we find the hidden "bridge" all is easy. And where is that bridge? Within, just beneath the surface appearance of things. For the truth is, the entire universe which is a net in which the ignorant are hopelessly caught, is also the way out to liberation. We just have to gain the right inner insight through meditation.

And how do we let the spirit move within us?

By *standing aside and letting him battle for thee.*

This entire cosmos is an evolutionary device that moves inexorably toward the revelation of God in all. It is a much greater travail than that of the body in childbearing, and it is painful in the superficial levels, but the result makes it all worthwhile and relatively easy. Inner divinity must be released. Just as Jesus in the tomb was wound around and around with linen bands stuck together in layers by more than one hundred pounds of gummy resins (John 19:39), so we are entangled and stuck up in the labyrinth of our earthly existence which includes all our previous incarnations, as well. Our spirits are like helpless mummies, lying in the tomb of the body and its material life. But, like Christ, they can pass through the bonds and be free. It is all a matter of letting the spirit live, of letting it breathe its source, the Holy Spirit, the Holy Breath of God.

Then it will be impossible for thee to strike one blow amiss.

How truly incredible, and how incredibly true. For some reason most people seem very afraid of making a mistake and either being laughed at and considered stupid or being condemned as a fool. It has amazed me through the years how reluctant nearly everyone is to answer questions put to them about what they perceive to be the truth. I cannot count the number of times I have had to assure students that there is no wrong answer, that my intention is to learn how they view something. No pronouncement of right or wrong is going to be made on it. Contradictorily, many people rush ahead and never give a thought to the wisdom or rightness of speech and action. How hard we work at tripping ourselves up where there really is no tangle at all.

Those who begin consciously looking after their spiritual development are particularly prone to fear of making a mistake, or taking a wrong turn, or wasting effort. But what else has been going on for lifetimes beyond number? So a few more false starts will not destroy us. The time comes when we have to drop the fear of being wrong and just plunge in and find out by the result what is wrong or right. The cosmos is a great laboratory of spiritual experimentation in which many mistakes will be made and quite a few explosions (some quite stinky) will occur. But so what? Better to be a spiritual scientist with smudges and smells on our white coat than to be locked in a straitjacket of fear and doubt. Go Ahead And Try! That should be our motto.

One of Swami Sivananda's created words was "mahafoolishity"—the condition of being maximally foolish. One of the stupidest things (and people) I ever saw was in Ranchi, Bihar (India), at the Ananda-mayi Ashram homeopathic dispensary run by my dear yogi friend Dr.

Mukherji. An old man came in who had married a girl about a third his age. He was carrying the product of the marriage, a fat, comotose little baby. Dr. Mukherji had prescribed a remedy for the child bride sight unseen since she claimed to be "too nervous" to come see him for herself. When he asked how the medicine was working, the old man said in a hollow sepulchral voice: "She has not taken that remedy." "Why not?" inquired the doctor, quite surprised. "Because she thinks she remembers somebody once told her that remedy was *hot*. And she cannot stand *hot* things." "No, no, it is not hot in the least," protested the doctor, "she should take it and benefit." "But she is afraid it might be *hot*," hooted the aged spouse, "so she will not take it. She wants you to give something else." Dr. Mukherji was kindly exasperated. "But that is the only medication for her problem. She must take it." "No, she is afraid it might be *hot*." Now this ring-around-the rosy went on and on, with "She is afraid it might be *hot*" recurring as the continual refrain. Finally the man stood up and left. Dr. Mukherji turned to me… and his look said it all. Then he turned back and began to laugh. And so did I. A wise response to the whole thing. In spiritual life we cannot be afraid that it might be "hot." Heaven and hell should both be disregarded: we must *move on*. Then we will not fail, ever.

But if thou look not for him, if thou pass him by, then there is no safe-guard for thee.

Absolutely! If we look not within (for "he" is nowhere else), but pass him by as we rush down the highways and byways of "life," not only will there be no safeguard for us, there is the absolute assurance of a collision and crack-up, just like in a few hundred or a thousand past lives. As a consequence:

Thy brain will reel, thy heart grow uncertain, and in the dust of the battlefield thy sight and senses will fail,…

Confusion, doubt, and imperception are the only possible outcome of turning from or ignoring the inner light of the spirit.

...and thou wilt not know thy friends from thy enemies.

This is the worst of the consequences that follow from rejecting or losing sight of spiritual realities. We become truly negative: everything is seen as opposite to what they really are, just as in a photographic negative the dark is light and the light is dark. Seeking to help ourselves, we can only come to harm, for we inevitably do that which compounds our trouble or adds some new dimension to it. (Any general textbook on psychology will reveal the truth of this.) In this state, a search for truth or God is inevitably perilous. This is why religion and religionists can be so harmful. The fault does not lie with religion itself or with the pursuit of spiritual life, but rather with those who are engaged in it. As Jesus pointed out, when the blind lead the blind they all fall into the ditch (Matthew 15:14). "Living in the abyss of ignorance yet wise in their own conceit, deluded fools go round and round, the blind led by the blind" (Katha Upanishad 1:2:5; Mundaka Upanishad 1.2.8).

"Where there is no vision, the people perish" (Proverbs 29:18). Without spiritual vision any spiritual endeavor is hopeless, and usually turns out to not be spiritual at all, but physical, emotional, or fantasy. This is why it is harmful to go around trying to force people into spiritual life or perspective. At best hypocrisy will result, and at worst spiritual harm for themselves and others will occur. This is why a true religion simply makes itself available, but never seeks to convert or convince. Conversion and conviction must arise from the spontaneous spiritual awakening that comes to all of us in time. God has eternity (and so do we) in which this can happen. There is no need for anxiety regarding others. The same illumination that has come forth in us is in them and shall shine forth when it should, not one moment more or less. It is all inward, and no outer force can effect that awakening. Nor can it prevent it.

For this reason we must be extremely careful of people or groups that are supposedly spiritual, for they many times are just the opposite. Not being truly of the spirit they become physically and mentally coercive, abusive and delusive. To those who are just beginning to wake up inwardly and stir to effective spiritual life, they can be extremely confusing and even destructive. To those who have become stabilized in their interior awakening they are only a pathetic joke, but it is not good to take chances with them. Caution is wisdom in relation to them—always. I am not counseling you to fear them, but to be wary of them. On your own you will discover that they are a waste of time at best.

In the same way, be careful about speaking of spiritual matters to those who may be unready for it or even (consciously or subconsciously) opposed to things of the spirit. Do not judge by appearances or take anyone's words at face value, especially the enthusiastic and emotional "glowies" who seem to radiate love, peace and light. They are also insightfuly called "Bliss Bunnies." This is usually a cover for just the opposite, or a self-delusion. So be careful, cautious and tread warily and softly in introducing spiritual subjects. Try to gauge just how real their spiritual awareness is, and to what degree they are awake.

Just as you do not discuss with a preschooler the ins and outs of the stock market or physics or higher mathematics, so do not burden them with what they are not capable of grasping. Pay no attention to their opinion of themselves or their aspiration. You must apply wisdom here and usually remain safely silent. Your ego may want to shine and strut in spiritual talk, but let that be a warning to you that not a word should be said lest you harm yourself.

Many times I have seen genuinely spiritual people dismissed by the shallow as ignorant and unspiritual because they kept quiet when they should. This happened to me one time in India when I visited a yogi that lived on an island in the Ganges. Because I would not ply him with "profound" questions, but simply sat and listened to him and three others play religious ring-around-the-rosy with words, he became very dissatisfied with me and hinted that I need not return to see him again.

Do not believe that you can help the ignorant and immature. Neither can you save them from harm if in their ignorance and immaturity they are blithely (and happily and self-satisfiedly) going in the wrong direction, even perhaps to harm and pain. This is their responsibility: they have *chosen* it. That is what free will is all about. Some people need to burn themselves to learn to avoid fire. Ego-based interference is not compassion. Keep your hands to yourself. God does; and he is wiser than us.

If we cannot tell our friends from our enemies, what shall we do? Look within, become established in the inner vision, and let our immortal spirit lead us. Do not sit around waiting for God to do the calling and the leading. Wake up, stand up and get moving.

Shake off childish conceptions and misperceptions about God and hearken to the truth the Master now says to you:

He is thyself, yet thou art but finite and liable to error. He is eternal and is sure. He is eternal truth.

These are truly the words of life. God is our own Self. He is eternal, we are eternal. He has never not existed, nor shall He ever cease to exist; and it is the same with us. We and God have existed co-eternally. There has never been separation between us to any degree whatsoever. He knows that, but we do not. We have lost that awareness, He has not. And we can regain it in Him, for He is the root of our root, the Spirit of our spirit. He is the Whole and we are the parts but nonetheless eternally divine. We are *one* with Him but we are not *the same* as He. He is infinite and not subject to error; we are finite and susceptible to error. We are eternal, as is he, but at present we are *un*sure, subject to coming and going, birth and death, rising and falling and a host of contradicting dualities. And this confusion will persist as long as we look to our finitude. But if we turn to Infinity, to God Who is eternal Truth, then the confusion will fade away, be seen as merely a mirage, and we, too, will become stable and Real.

We have come to believe that eternity is merely time without end and that truth is a conglomerate of the right or correct ideas. Consequently we never even touch either eternity or truth. But the Master now lets us know that eternity and truth are God Himself. We cannot enter eternity or find truth. Rather we can wake up in God (where we have always been), in eternity, in truth. At the moment we think we are "lost" or "strayed" from God, but that is an illusion. When we awake from this dream of separation, fear and doubt are ended forever, for:

When once he has entered thee and become thy warrior, he will never utterly desert thee, and at the day of the great peace he will become one with thee.

We are always one with God, as the Master has assured us, but we do not know that. Actually we forget it utterly. But in time, through cultivation of inner consciousness, we begin to experience that unity to a slight degree, and it increases in us much as does the light of day: in stages. Then the full light comes in "the day of the great peace" when everything but God ceases to exist in our perception.

Spiritual sight comes in steps as exact as the ascent of a ladder: one by one, and each following the other in precise order. This is not a haphazard ascent, and has nothing to do with the vague muddle of popular religious thought or devotion. It is a methodology of the spirit and has nothing to do with either the ideas of the seeker or the whims of a conditioned deity. It is the only real science there is, for it alone results in Knowledge and Truth: God. Yoga is its name.

5. Listen to the song of life.

6. Store in your memory the melody you hear.

7. Learn from it the lesson of harmony.

Though spiritual life is largely based on the cultivation of intuition, some things are required of the intellect: be objective; note and remember; reflect and learn. Then apply what has been learned in the manner that will achieve harmony. It cannot be denied that a great deal of people learn from life how to exploit it, distort it or turn it to misery for others and often for themselves. All knowledge is a two-edged sword that cuts both ways. So it is imperative for us to use it skillfully, as Buddha pointed out.

Life itself teaches us how to live. When you have learned the lesson:

8. You can stand upright now, firm as a rock amid the turmoil, obeying the warrior who is thyself and thy king. Unconcerned in the battle save to do his bidding, having no longer any care as to the result of the battle, for one thing only is important, that the warrior shall win, and you know he is incapable of defeat—standing thus, cool and awakened, use the hearing you have acquired by pain and by the destruction of pain. Only fragments of the great song come to your ears while yet you are but man. But if you listen to it, remember it faithfully, so that none which has reached you is lost, and endeavor to learn from it the meaning of the mystery which surrounds you. In time you will need no teacher. For as the individual has voice, so has that in which the individual exists. Life itself has speech and is never silent. And its utterance is not, as you that are deaf may suppose,

a cry: it is a song. Learn from it that you are part of the harmony; learn from it to obey the laws of the harmony.

We can see right away that this is a list of characteristics we will have, not what we will have to still attain, once we have met our true Self and known it to be both us and God.

Unconcerned in the battle save to do his bidding, having no longer any care as to the result of the battle, for one thing only is important, that the warrior shall win, and you know he is incapable of defeat....

The Master is telling us to be unconcerned in the battle because we know victory is assured. So we can take our eyes off the result and keep them on God alone Who is the cause.

...standing thus, cool and awakened,....

What a beautiful picture is presented to us: a warrior cool amidst the heat of battle because he is *awakened*: awakened to the truth that it is all a dream, a dream of God, but nonetheless a dream from which we can all awaken into fearlessness. In one sense we will not win the battle, we will awaken from it. What joy, what freedom, what release! Yet we will still be in the dream, though awake in a state that transcends it. We are no more "of the dream" than is God, the Dreamer, yet, like him, we are to remain involved in it until perfection in dreaming is achieved.

...use the hearing you have acquired by pain and by the destruction of pain. "Ears to hear" (Matthew 11:15) are not easy to come by. They are trophies won only after long and arduous battle.

The Master shows that we have to undergo two forms of involvement with pain: we must incur pain by struggle and eliminate pain by struggle. The first comes before wisdom begins its rise in us, and the second follows that arising "as does night the day." But pain is the gateway to hearing in the spirit. We are usually nettled by all the exoteric Christian talk about the cross and the way of the cross, but no matter how little the speakers may understand their words, they are the truth (though misunderstood by them) and must become both our experience and our wisdom.

Only fragments of the great song come to your ears while yet you are but man. But if you listen to it, remember it faithfully, so that none which has reached you is lost, and endeavor to learn from it the meaning of the mystery which surrounds you.

How sublime this all is, and thoroughly true, and how brilliantly the Master illumines the way and guides us around all pitfalls.

It is true that those in the human condition cannot perceive the entire song of life; but that does not mean that we should wait until we hear the whole melody before learning from it and gaining understanding from it. If we retain and use that which comes to us, however fragmentary it may be, that itself will begin to transform us and move us onward to the complete message. The Master is also showing us that simply being in awe of creation or of the vastness of spirit is worth little; and so is just looking at everything in reverence as a mystery. It all has meaning and its script must be deciphered. And the more we comprehend the more we will learn. God did not spread forth the cosmos to impress us or to merely indicate that he exists. It has a purpose, and that purpose is *learning*. Wandering the cosmos from life to life like a tourist, just looking and admiring, is not our purpose, nor does attributing it all to God or praising Him for it mean anything. We have to study it and learn. Creation is a preparatory school for divinity.

In time you will need no teacher. For as the individual has voice, so has that in which the individual exists.

The ego of human beings paints them into two corners: false independence and false dependence. When we still need to learn from outer sources, especially other human beings, the ego screams that we need no teacher, that we are sufficient of ourselves to learn and understand. Though this will be true for us in time, when adopted too soon this can completely destroy our spiritual life. I have seen it many times.

On the other hand, once we do start coming into our own in spiritual growth, and we need to start developing the capacity for analyzing and learning on our own and gaining the self-reliance ultimately needed in the spiritual battle, our ego either belittles us and badgers us into thinking that we are stupid and incompetent, or it gets very religious and starts babbling about "making God our all" and realizing that God is the only power in the universe, that we must realize we are his children and that he does all for us that is needful; that "surrender" and "trust" and "relying on God alone" are the marks of love and faith. "Let go and let God" becomes the motto. Having been raised on this sentimental foolishness, it was a revelation and a relief when I read in the Gita the words of Krishna to Arjuna: "Stand up resolved to fight" (Bhagavad Gita 2:37).

So, "in the fullness of time" we must stand on our own. Not that we reject the past teachings we have received, but that having learned the theory it is now time to move on to demonstration of it in our own life. This, too, is one of the lessons God has intended for us. At the same time we realize that it is indeed His power alone that does all things, that it is His wisdom alone that can shine forth in us; that it is His will that we reach out and wield that power and wisdom He is making so freely accessible to us. When we do this we realize that God truly is acting and ascending through us. That it is our willingness that must be put forth by us. God, in whom we as individuals exist, begins to speak to us from within rather than from without, and becomes our teacher, but not until we develop the self-reliance that mirrors His own self-sufficiency.

Life itself has speech and is never silent. And its utterance is not, as you that are deaf may suppose, a cry: it is a song. Learn from it that you are part of the harmony; learn from it to obey the laws of the harmony.

This is somewhat of a recapitulation to drive the point home. Life is not chaotic or happenstance: it is pattern and purpose. An illiterate person sees writing as meaningless scratches, but the literate read a message.

9. Regard earnestly all the life that surrounds you.

Life that surrounds us is as much an extension of us as it is an extension of God's Being. Contrary to usual "spiritual" thinking, it is not antithetical to us nor really a distraction: that is brought about by our mishandling and misperceiving of it. The plain truth is that when we have gained sufficient interior opening, we will find that by comprehending our life we comprehend ourselves. Our outer life is a mirror of our inner state, and not just in the matter of karma. The entire character and tone of our life indicates the character and inner tone of our state of consciousness. As the Chinese say: "When mean-spirited people live behind the door, mean-spirited people come before the door." When life opposes us, it is because we oppose ourselves. When outer situations make it hard or impossible to accomplish something it is sometimes (though not always) because inwardly we do not want to do so. No one is a victim of life. Life really is what we make it. That is a bitter lesson for the ego, but one we must learn. It is, however, a joyful insight for the spirit, because it means we can transform our life by changing ourselves.

But it always works from the inside out. That is the first law of harmony. Once we learn that, the others will be rapidly recognized. Therefore, "regard earnestly all the life that surrounds you" for it *is* you. Furthermore, *all* life must be regarded earnestly, not just the part that appeals to us. Everything must be taken into account, for everything is a figure in the ledger book of our life. We will not get the right total if we turn from anything whatsoever. People who refuse to confront or admit the negative in their outward life are trying to deny the negativity of their inner life.

10. Learn to look intelligently into the hearts of men.

Since we live with people, we must come to comprehend them, to look beyond their outer shell and into their hearts, to see the profound depths that they themselves do not see. Of course both good and bad are there, but we need to see what forces are operating in the hearts of those around us, to realize what is happening to them at the moment, and to understand them. This does not mean that we will passively accept them or think that everything is just fine with them. If they were not in drastic need they would not even be here in this world of samsara.

And God intends for us to save ourselves. Until we face up to that we will get nowhere. Again, saying it is all up to God is nonsense. The Master is preparing us for good sense. So then he says:

11. Regard most earnestly your own heart.
12. For through your own heart comes the one light which can illuminate life and make it clear to your eyes. Study the hearts of men, that you may know what is that world in which you live and of which you will to be a part. Regard the constantly changing and moving life which surrounds you, for it is formed by the hearts of men; and as you learn to understand their constitution and meaning, you will by degrees be able to read the larger word of life.

Regard most earnestly your own heart. For through your own heart comes the one light which can illuminate life and make it clear to your eyes.
In Patanjali's Yoga Sutras, the foundation text of Yoga, self-study (*swadhyaya*) is stated to be a prime requisite. We must soberly and continually watch over our heart—our inner mind. Although a lot that is worthless or negative may come from the heart, at the bottom are the

wellsprings of spirit. And at that bottom "comes the one light which can illuminate life and make it clear to your eyes." We are indeed supposed to see all the ego-rubbish, in the form of both vice and virtue, and acknowledge and deal with it, but we are also to keep on digging and clearing until the light of the One shines forth.

Study the hearts of men, that you may know what is that world in which you live and of which you will to be a part. Regard the constantly changing and moving life which surrounds you, for it is formed by the hearts of men; and as you learn to understand their constitution and meaning, you will by degrees be able to read the larger word of life.

This needs no comment, except it should be pointed out that the Master does not say we are caught in life or thrust into it by forces external to ourselves, not even God. He states flatly that we *will* to be a part of this world. If we do not like our involvement in the world, either the involvement itself or the form it is taking, we need only change our will.

13. Speech comes only with knowledge. Attain to knowledge and you will attain to speech.

Oh, if only the "teachers" of this world would adopt this principle! It shows us how people can speak volumes and really say nothing, and some people can remain silent and teach volumes.

"It shall even be as when an hungry man dreameth, and, behold, he eateth; but he awaketh, and his soul is empty: or as when a thirsty man dreameth, and, behold, he drinketh; but he awaketh, and, behold, he is faint, and his soul hath appetite" (Isaiah 29:8). This is also true of most seekers who have come into the orbit of ignorant instructors, especially spiritual ones. No matter how much they cram in lectures, books and seminars, they remain spiritually starved or even deluded. By far most "spiritual teachers" speak emptiness from an empty heart.

Attain to knowledge and you will attain to speech. This is not poetry; I once witnessed this myself. I used to attend a yoga center that had Sunday morning lectures given by two speakers: one remarkably good and the other remarkably poor. They alternated Sundays, and being loyal I never missed a talk, so I sat through a lot of painfully bad ones. Then one Sunday the poor speaker announced that for the next few weeks he would be on a meditation retreat. Happy news! For more than a month I would not suffer through his bumbling talks. But in time the Sunday came when he was going to speak again. So I fortified myself with determination and went, already squirming. But all was changed. His talk was magnificent. And from then on all his talks were quite good. Obviously he had experienced a spiritual breakthrough in his weeks of meditation, and it affected his speaking ability.

It is our ignorance that we need deliverance from. Many people like to make excuse about neglecting spiritual life, blaming their spouse, environment, parents, job, economic situation, society and whatnot. But the truth is: we alone are our problem, and we need to be saved from our (false) selves.

14. Having obtained the use of the inner senses, having conquered the desires of the outer senses, having conquered the desires of the individual soul, and having obtained knowledge, prepare now, O disciple, to enter upon the way in reality. The path is found: make yourself ready to tread it.

The crucial expression here is "in reality." Many (most) enter the path in imagination only. I have never heard a person speak of "being on the path" for many years who was not hopelessly caught in his own self-fantasy, far, far away from the possibility of even coming in sight of The Way. Spiritually incompetent people abound who believe they are leaving their bodies nightly for "work on the higher planes," who believe that through past ages they have been returning to earth again and again to uplift humanity under the aegis of "the Masters." The lesser they really are, the more grandiose their delusions. The three reincarnated Jesus Christs I have encountered at least were crazy enough to have strong personalities. The "channelers" have at least found their niche, capable of being nothing more than telephones for discarnate beings as pointless as themselves.

The Master lists the qualities which are necessary before we can even start to get ready to enter the path. They are:

1) Development of the inner, psychic senses.

2) Elimination of the desires arising from the outer material senses.

3) Elimination of the desires arising from ego-identity and its resulting erroneous concept of individuality

4) Possession of true knowledge.

These traits are not the marks of saints or liberated beings, they are required just to start getting ready to start on the path. Now, there are multitudes of "ways" we can travel that require none of these things, and many demand their opposites. But the true way cannot be approached without them.

Two principles are implied here that we should not miss. First, only those who have entered the inner world can control their life in the outer world. To badger people to "stop doing that" rather than showing them how to grow beyond "that" is stupid and sadistic. If we cannot show the way beyond (and I do not mean "getting saved" or "giving it all over to the Lord") then we should leave others alone and find out the way and ourselves "get beyond" before we presume to advise them. Second, the dissolution of egoic motivations has to occur before real knowledge can be obtained. Information and misinformation we can get in floods, and shall until egotism is eliminated (not just suppressed or put out to pasture). One reason it is hard to find a worthy teacher is the fact that worthy teachers are quiet and humble, never putting themselves forward, and we who are blinded by egotism are incapable of seeing them for what they really are. We usually consider them dull, narrow and tiresome.

How do we prepare to enter the path? The Master does not leave us guessing.

15. Inquire of the earth, the air, and the water, of the secrets they hold for you. The development of your inner senses will enable you to do this.

Whatever we see is but the outermost layer of a vast series of increasingly subtle levels of being. When the inner senses are developed we become able to penetrate into those levels. When the subtlest senses of the causal level are developed we are able to perceive the ideational level of things, to comprehend them as concepts and to read the basic script of the cosmos. The Master is referring to this. The perceptions that arise before then may be subtle and intriguing, but they yield no "secrets," no wisdom, only knowledge of phenomena and their manipulation. This is a labyrinth in which we become easily lost and confused, so it is best to keep away from it. Occultism quickly opens this and entices us into exploration that ultimately leads nowhere. We must turn from the phenomena and seek only the meaning of things.

16. Inquire of the holy ones of the earth of the secrets they hold for you. The conquering of the desires of the outer senses will give you the right to do this.

Knowledge received without the seeker first being established in spiritual consciousness can be detrimental. Firstly, because it can be misunderstood and therefore wrongly applied. Further, the ego eagerly grasps at whatever it can use to assert itself and extend its dominion. When all desire for the outer levels has been eliminated, not just suppressed or controlled, only then is higher knowledge safe for us.

176

"The holy ones of the earth" are multiform. Some are enlightened human beings, some are guardian spirits of earth life, some are the patterns of earthly existence: blueprints of creative forces. Others are the states of awareness inherent in earthly phenomena. In this inquiry the nature of all things as pure consciousness is revealed and the seeker begins to realize and manifest that truth. It is this attainment which enables a person to change water into wine, move mountains, and alter the patterns of life which we call birth, disease, and death. It is the expansion into omniscience and omnipotence. Still, this is all outer-oriented, however subtle or glorious. So the Master continues:

17. Inquire of the inmost, the one, of its final secret which it holds for you through the ages.

The great and difficult victory, the conquering of the desires of the individual soul, is a work of ages; therefore expect not to obtain its reward until ages of experience have been accumulated. When the time of learning this seventeenth rule is reached, man is on the threshold of becoming more than man.

The final secret is perfect Self-knowledge and Self-manifestation. It transcends all that has gone before. It is the revelation of the Eternal which forever negates the temporal. To say more would be to cloud the matter.

Now the Master would caution those who think that the mere willing will guarantee the attaining. Their enthusiasm, if indulged, will in time turn to disgust and disbelief, for it is based on a mistaken view both of themselves and the goal. The prime error is the conviction that enlightenment is at hand for the picking up. Just wish for it... and it is yours. So he tells us: "The great and difficult victory, the conquering of the desires of the individual soul, is a work of ages; therefore expect not to obtain its reward until ages of experience have been accumulated.

When the time of learning this seventeenth rule is reached, man is on the threshold of becoming more than man."

He is giving us a dual message. Only after many ages can the final victory be won. Therefore we must have the experience of ages before we can engage in that final battle. However, we would not learn this truth unless we already had accumulated most of it. And that fact tells us that we are even now "on the threshold of becoming more than man."

We have come a long way together in this commentary. Consequently I am going to end by relaying to you the final words of the Master without comment, for they cannot be illumined by more words. Simply read and understand.

18. The knowledge which is now yours is only yours because your soul has become one with all pure souls and with the inmost. It is a trust vested in you by the Most High. Betray it, misuse your knowledge, or neglect it, and it is possible even now for you to fall from the high estate you have attained. Great ones fall back, even from the threshold, unable to sustain the weight of their responsibility, unable to pass on. Therefore look forward always with awe and trembling to this moment, and be prepared for the battle.

19. It is written that for him who is on the threshold of divinity no law can be framed, no guide can exist. Yet to enlighten the disciple, the final struggle may be thus expressed:

Hold fast to that which has neither substance nor existence.

20. Listen only to the voice which is soundless.

21. Look only on that which is invisible alike to the inner and outer sense.

PEACE BE WITH YOU.

Introduction to Soham Yoga

I–The Practice of Soham Yoga Meditation

1) Sit upright, comfortable and relaxed, with your hands on your knees or thighs or resting, one on the other, in your lap.

2) Turn your eyes slightly downward and close them gently. This removes visual distractions and reduces your brain-wave activity by about seventy-five percent, thus helping to calm the mind. During meditation your eyes may move upward and downward naturally of their own accord. This is as it should be when it happens spontaneously. But start out with them turned slightly downward without any strain.

3) Be aware of your breath naturally (automatically) flowing in and out. Your mouth should be closed so that all breathing is done through the nose. This also aids in quieting the mind. Though your mouth is closed, the jaw muscles should be relaxed so the upper and lower teeth are not clenched or touching one another, but parted. Breathe naturally, spontaneously. Your breathing should always be easeful and natural, not deliberate or artificial.

4) Then in a very quiet and gentle manner begin *mentally* intoning Soham in time with your breathing. (Remember: Soham is pronounced like our English words *So* and *Hum*.)

Intone *Soooooo*, prolonging a single intonation throughout each inhalation, and *Huuummm*, prolonging a single intonation throughout each exhalation, "singing" the syllables on a single note.

There is no need to pull or push the mind. Let your relaxed attention sink into and get absorbed in the mental sound of your inner intonings of Soham.

Fit the intonations to the breath–not the breath to the intonations. If the breath is short, then the intonation should be short. If the breath is long, then the intonation should be long. It does not matter if the inhalations and exhalations are not of equal length. Whatever is natural and spontaneous is what is right.

Your intonation of *Soooooo* should begin when your inhalation begins, and *Huuummm* should begin when your exhalation begins. In this way your intonations should be virtually continuous, that is:

SoooooHuuummmSoooooHuuummmSoooooHuuummm.

Do not torture yourself about this–basically continuous is good enough.

5) For the rest of your meditation time keep on intoning Soham in time with your breath, calmly listening to the mental sound.

6) In Soham meditation we do not deliberately concentrate on any particular point of the body such as the third eye, as we want the subtle energies of Soham to be free to manifest themselves as is best at the moment. However, as you meditate you may become aware of one or more areas of your brain or body at different times. This is all right when such sensations come and go spontaneously, but keep centered on your intonations of Soham in time with your breath.

7) In time your inner mental intonations of Soham may change to a more mellow or softer form, even to an inner whispering that is almost silent, but the syllables are always fully present and effective. Your intonations may even become silent, like a soundless mouthing of Soham or just the thought or movement of Soham, yet you will still be intoning Soham in your intention. And of this be sure: *Soham never ceases.* Never. You may find that your intonations of Soham move back and forth from more objective to more subtle and

back to more objective. Just intone in the manner that is natural at the moment.

8) In the same way you will find that your breath will also become more subtle and refined, and slow down. Sometimes the breath may not be perceived as movement of the lungs, but just as the subtle pranic energy movement which causes the physical breath. Your breath can even become so light that it seems as though you are not breathing at all, just *thinking* the breath (or almost so).

9) Thoughts, impressions, memories, inner sensations, and suchlike may also arise during meditation. Be calmly aware of all these things in a detached and objective manner, but keep your attention centered in your intonations of Soham in time with your breath. Do not let your attention become centered on or caught up in any inner or outer phenomena. Be calmly aware of all these things in a detached and objective manner. They are part of the transforming work of Soham, and are perfectly all right, but keep your attention centered in your intonations of Soham in time with your breath. Even though something feels very right or good when it occurs, it should not be forced or hung on to. The sum and substance of it all is this: It is not the experience we are after, but the effect. Also, since we are all different, no one can say exactly what a person's experiences in meditation are going to be like.

10) Soham japa and meditation can make us aware of the subtle levels of our being, many of which are out of phase with one another and are either confused or reversed in their polarity. The japa and meditation correct these things, but sometimes, especially at the beginning of meditation, we can experience these aberrations as uncomfortable or uneasy sensations, a feeling or heaviness or stasis or other peculiar sensations that are generally uncomfortable and somehow feel "not right." When this occurs, do not try to interfere with it or "make it better." Rather, just relax, keep on with the japa/meditation, calmly aware and let it be as it is. In time the problem in the subtle energy levels will be corrected

and the feeling will become easy and pleasant. Simple as the practice is, it has deep and far-reaching effects, as you will see for yourself.

11) If you find yourself getting restless, distracted, fuzzy, anxious or tense in any degree, just take a deep breath and let it out fully, feeling that you are releasing and breathing out all tensions, and continue as before.

12) Remember: Soham Yoga meditation basically consists of four things: a) sitting with the eyes closed; b) being aware of our breath as it moves in and out; c) mentally intoning Soham in time with the breath; and d) listening to those mental intonations: all in a relaxed and easeful manner, without strain.

Breath and sound are the two major spiritual powers possessed by us, so they are combined for Soham Yoga practice. It is very natural to intone Soham in time with the breathing. It is simple and easy.

13) At the end of your meditation time, keep on intoning Soham in time with your breath as you go about your various activities, listening to the inner mantric sound, just as in meditation. One of the cardinal virtues of Soham sadhana is its capacity to be practiced throughout the day. The *Yoga Rasyanam* in verse 303 says: "Before and after the regular [meditation] practice, the repetition of Soham should be continuously done [in time with the breath] while walking, sitting or even sleeping.... This leads to ultimate success."

Can it be that simple and easy? Yes, because it goes directly to the root of our bondage which is a single—and therefore simple—thing: loss of awareness. Soham is the seed (bija) mantra of nirvanic consciousness. You take a seed, put it in the soil, water it and the sun does the rest. You plant the seed of Soham in your inner consciousness through japa and meditation and both your Self and the Supreme Self do the rest. By intentionally intoning *So* and *Ham* with the breath we are linking the conscious with superconscious mind, bringing the superconscious onto the conscious level and merging them until they become one. This is what the Bhagavad Gita (6:29) means by the term yoga-yukta–joined to yoga. It is divinely simple!

The secret of success is regularity in meditation. "A diamond is a piece of coal that never gave up." If you meditate regularly, every day, great will be the result. Water, though the softest substance known, can wear through the hardest stone by means of a steady dripping. In the old story of the tortoise and the hare, the tortoise won the race because he kept at it steadily, whereas the hare ran in spurts. He ran much faster then the tortoise, but the irregularity of his running made him lose the race. Meditation keeps moving onward in its effect when regularly practiced, producing steady growth through steady practice. The more we walk the farther we travel; the more we meditate the nearer and quicker we draw to the goal.

The four elements of Soham Yoga meditation

There are four components of Soham Yoga meditation:

1) sitting with closed eyes;

2) being aware of the breath as it moves in and out;

3) mentally intoning Soham in time with the breathing;

4) listening to the inner, mental intonations of Soham and becoming absorbed in the subtle sound.

These are the essential ingredients of Soham Yoga meditation, and we should confine our attention to them. If in meditation we feel unsure as to whether things are going right, we need only check to see if these four things are being done and our attention is centered in them. If so, all is well. If not, it is a simple matter to return to them and make everything right. Success in Soham Yoga consists of going deeper and deeper into the subtle sound of the Soham mantra as we intone it within. It is the thread leading us into the center of Reality.

Gorakhnath summed up his Soham Yoga practice and its effect in this manner: "The mind is the root and the breath is the branch; the sound [of Soham] is the guru and attention [to the sound] is the disciple. With the essence called deliverance [*nirvana tattwa*–the principle of liberation] Gorakhnath wanders about, himself in himself" (Gorakh Bodha 10).

Invariables

There are certain invariables of Soham Yoga meditation.

1) We always meditate with closed mouth and eyes.

2) We always mentally intone Soham in time with the breath.

3) Our mental intonations of Soham, like the breath to which we are linking them, should be virtually continuous, not with long breaks between them. That is: *SooooooHuuummmSooooooHuuummmSoooooo-HuuummmSooooooHuuummm*. (Basically continuous is good enough.)

4) The inner, mental, intonations of Soham never cease. Never. We must not let passivity or heaviness of mind interrupt our intonations by pulling us into negative silence. That would be a descent rather than an ascent.

5) The focus, the center of attention, of our meditation is the sound of our mental intonations of Soham in time with our breath. In an easeful and relaxed manner we become absorbed in that inner sound.

6) Our mental intonations of Soham are gentle, quiet and subtle.

For more information on Soham Yoga,
visit our website:

OCOY.ORG

GLOSSARY

Antahkarana: Internal instrument; the subtle bodies; fourfold mind: mind, intellect, ego and subconscious mind.

Arjuna: The great disciple of Krishna, who imparted to him the teachings found in the Bhagavad Gita. The third of the Pandava brothers who were major figures in the Mahabharata War. His name literally means "bright," "white" or "clear."

Avatar(a): A fully liberated spirit (jiva) who is born into a world below Satya Loka to help others attain liberation. Though commonly referred to as a divine incarnation, an avatar actually is totally one with God, and therefore an incarnation of God-Consciousness.

Bhagavad Gita: "The Song of God." The sacred philosophical text often called "the Hindu Bible," part of the epic Mahabharata by Vyasa; the most popular sacred text in Hinduism.

Brahman: The Absolute Reality; the Truth proclaimed in the Upanishads; the Supreme Reality that is one and indivisible, infinite, and eternal; all-pervading, changeless Existence; Existence-knowledge-bliss Absolute (Satchidananda); Absolute Consciousness; it is not only all-powerful but all-power itself; not only all-knowing and blissful but all-knowledge and all-bliss itself.

Gita: Song; The Bhagavad Gita.

Japa: Repetition of a mantra.

Jnana: Knowledge; knowledge of Reality–of Brahman, the Absolute; also denotes the process of reasoning by which the Ultimate Truth is attained. The word is generally used to denote the knowledge by which one is aware of one's identity with Brahman.

Karma: Karma, derived from the Sanskrit root *kri*, which means to act, do, or make, means any kind of action, including thought and feeling. It also means the effects of action. Karma is both action and reaction, the metaphysical equivalent of the principle: "For every action there is an equal and opposite reaction." "Whatsoever a man soweth, that shall he also reap" (Galatians 6:7). It is karma operating through the law of cause and effect that binds the jiva or the individual soul to the wheel of birth and death. There are three forms of karma: sanchita, agami, and prarabdha. Sanchita karma is the vast store of accumulated actions done in the past, the fruits of which have not yet been reaped. Agami karma is the action that will be done by the individual in the future. Prarabdha karma is the action that has begun to fructify, the fruit of which is being reaped in this life.

Kauravas: The opponents of the Pandavas in the Mahabharata War, led by Duryodhana.

Krishna: An avatar born in India about three thousand years ago, Whose teachings to His disciple Arjuna on the eve of the Great India (Mahabharata) War comprise the Bhagavad Gita.

Mahabharata: The world's longest epic poem (110,00 verses) about the Mahabharata (Great Indian) War that took place about three thousand years ago. The Mahabharata also includes the Bhagavad Gita, the most popular sacred text of Hinduism.

Mahatma: Literally: "a great soul [atma]." Usually a designation for a sannyasi, sage or saint.

Mantra(m): Sacred syllable or word or set of words through the repetition and reflection of which one attains perfection or realization of the Self. Literally, "a transforming thought" (manat trayate). A mantra, then is a sound formula that transforms the consciousness.

Niyama: Observance; the five Do's of Yoga: 1) Shaucha: purity, cleanliness; 2) Santosha: contentment, peacefulness; 3) Tapas: austerity, practical (i.e., result-producing) spiritual discipline; 4) Swadhyaya: self-study, spiritual study; 5) Ishwarapranidhana: offering of one's life to God.

Pandavas: The five sons of King Pandu: Yudhishthira, Bhima, Arjuna, Nakula, and Sahadeva. Their lives are described in the Mahabharata.

Parabrahman: Supreme Brahman.

Paramatma(n): The Supreme Self, God.

Parameshwara: The Supreme (Param) Lord (Ishwara).

Ramakrishna, Sri: Sri Ramakrishna lived in India in the second half of the nineteenth century, and is regarded by all India as a perfectly enlightened person–and by many as an Incarnation of God.

Sadhana: Spiritual practice.

Samsara: Life through repeated births and deaths; the wheel of birth and death; the process of earthly life.

Samsara chakra: The wheel of birth and death.

Samsari: The transmigrating soul.

Samsaric: Having to do with samsara; involved with samsara; partaking of the traits or qualities of samsara.

Samsarin: One who is subject to samsara–repeated births and deaths–and who is deluded by its appearances, immersed in ignorance.

Samskara: Impression in the mind, either conscious or subconscious, produced by action or experience in this or previous lives; propensities of the mental residue of impressions; subliminal activators; prenatal tendency. See Vasana.

Shishya: Disciple; student.

Siddha: A perfected–liberated–being, an adept, a seer, a perfect yogi.

Soham: "That am I;" the ultimate Atma mantra, the mantra of the Self; the Ajapa Gayatri formula of meditation in which "So" is intoned mentally during natural inhalation and "Ham" is intoned mentally during natural exhalation. Soham is pronounced "Sohum," as the short "a" in Sanskrit is pronounced like the American "u" in "up."

Soham Bhava: The state of being and awareness: "THAT I am." Gorakhnath says that So'ham Bhava includes total Self-comprehension (ahamta), total Self-mastery (akhanda aishwarya), unbroken awareness of the unity of the Self (swatmata), awareness of the unity of the Self with all phenomenal existence–as the Self (vishwanubhava), knowledge of all within and without the Self–united in the Self (sarvajñatwa).

Swadhyaya: Introspective self-study or self-analysis leading to self-understanding. Study of spiritual texts regarding the Self.

Swayamprakash(a): Self-luminous; self-illumined.

Vasana: Subtle desire; a tendency created in a person by the doing of an action or by experience; it induces the person to repeat the action or to seek a repetition of the experience; the subtle impression in the mind capable of developing itself into action; it is the cause of birth and experience in general; an aggregate or bundle of samskaras–the impressions of actions that remain unconsciously in the mind.

Vasudeva: "He who dwells in all things"–the Universal God.

Vedanta: Literally, "the end of the Vedas;" the Upanishads; the school of Hindu thought, based primarily on the Upanishads, upholding the doctrine of either pure non-dualism or conditional non-dualism. The original text of this school is Vedanta-darshana, the Brahma Sutras compiled by the sage Vyasa.

Vivekananda (Swami): The chief disciple of Sri Ramakrishna, who brought the message of Vedanta to the West at the end of the nineteenth century.

Yama: Restraint; the five Don'ts of Yoga: 1) ahimsa–non-violence, non-injury, harmlessness; 2) satya–truthfulness, honesty; 3) asteya–non-stealing, honesty, non-misappropriativeness; 4) brahmacharya–continence; 5) aparigraha–non-possessiveness, non-greed, non-selfishness, non-acquisitiveness. These five are called the Great Vow (Observance, Mahavrata) in the Yoga Sutras.

Yoga: Literally, "joining" or "union" from the Sanskrit root yuj. Union with the Supreme Being, or any practice that makes for such union. Meditation that unites the individual spirit with God, the Supreme Spirit. The name of the philosophy expounded by the sage Patanjali, teaching the process of union of the individual with the Universal Soul.

Yogananda (Paramhansa): The most influential yogi of the twentieth century in the West, author of *Autobiography of a Yogi* and founder of Self-Realization Fellowship in America.

Yogic: Having to do with Yoga.

ABOUT THE AUTHOR

Swami Nirmalananda Giri (Abbot George Burke) is the founder and director of the Light of the Spirit Monastery (Atma Jyoti Ashram) in Cedar Crest, New Mexico, USA.

In his many pilgrimages to India, he had the opportunity of meeting some of India's greatest spiritual figures, including Swami Sivananda of Rishikesh and Anandamayi Ma. During his first trip to India he was made a member of the ancient Swami Order by Swami Vidyananda Giri, a direct disciple of Paramhansa Yogananda, who had himself been given sannyas by the Shankaracharya of Puri, Jagadguru Bharati Krishna Tirtha.

In the United States he also encountered various Christian saints, including Saint John Maximovich of San Francisco and Saint Philaret Voznesensky of New York.

For many years Swami Nirmalananda has researched the identity of Jesus Christ and his teachings with India and Sanatana Dharma, including Yoga. It is his conclusion that Jesus lived in India for most of his life, and was a yogi and Sanatana Dharma missionary to the West. After his resurrection he returned to India and lived the rest of his life in the Himalayas.

He has written extensively on these and other topics, many of which are posted at OCOY.org.

Atma Jyoti Ashram
(Light of the Spirit Monastery)

Atma Jyoti Ashram (Light of the Spirit Monastery) is a monastic community for those men who seek direct experience of the Spirit through yoga meditation, traditional yogic discipline, Sanatana Dharma and the life of the sannyasi in the tradition of the Order of Shankara. Our lineage is in the Giri branch of the Order.

The public outreach of the monastery is through its website, OCOY.org (Original Christianity and Original Yoga). There you will find many articles on Original Christianity and Original Yoga, including *The Christ of India*. *Foundations of Yoga* and *How to Be a Yogi* are practical guides for anyone seriously interested in living the Yoga Life.

You will also discover many other articles on leading an effective spiritual life, including *Soham Yoga: The Yoga of the Self* and *Spiritual Benefits of a Vegetarian Diet*, as well as the "Dharma for Awakening" series—in-depth commentaries on these spiritual classics: the Bhagavad Gita, the Upanishads, the Dhammapada, the Tao Teh King and more.

You can listen to podcasts by Swami Nirmalananda on meditation, the Yoga Life, and remarkable spiritual people he has met in India and elsewhere, at http://ocoy.org/podcasts/

Join over 29,000 subscribers and watch over 200 videos on these topics and more, including recordings of online satsangs where Swami Nirmalananda answers various questions on practical aspects of spiritual life. A new series of talks on the Bhagavad Gita have also been added.

Visit our Youtube channel here:

Youtube.com/@lightofthespirit

Reading for Awakening

Light of the Spirit Press presents books on spiritual wisdom and Original Christianity and Original Yoga. From our "Dharma for Awakening" series (practical commentaries on the world's scriptures) to books on how to meditate and live a successful spiritual life, you will find books that are informative, helpful, and even entertaining.

Light of the Spirit Press is the publishing house of Light of the Spirit Monastery (Atma Jyoti Ashram) in Cedar Crest, New Mexico, USA. Our books feature the writings of the founder and director of the monastery, Swami Nirmalananda Giri (Abbot George Burke) which are also found on the monastery's website, OCOY.org.

We invite you to explore our publications in the following pages.

Find out more about our publications at
lightofthespiritpress.com

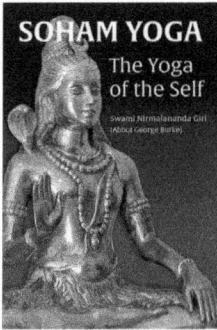

Soham Yoga
The Yoga of the Self

A complete and in-depth guide to effective meditation and the life that supports it, this important book explains with clarity and insight what real yoga is, and why and how to practice Soham Yoga meditation.

Discovered centuries ago by the Nath yogis, this simple and classic approach to self-realization has no "secrets," requires no "initiation," and is easily accessible to the serious modern yogi.

Includes helpful, practical advice on leading an effective spiritual life and many Illuminating quotes on Soham from Indian scriptures and great yogis.

"This book is a complete spiritual path." –Arnold Van Wie

Light of Soham
The Life and Teachings of Sri Gajanana Maharaj of Nashik

Gajanan Murlidhar Gupte, later known as Gajanana Maharaj, led an unassuming life, to all appearances a normal unmarried man of contemporary society. Crediting his personal transformation to the practice of the Soham mantra, he freely shared this practice with a small number of disciples, whom he simply called his friends. Strictly avoiding the trap of gurudom, he insisted that his friends be self-reliant and not be dependent on him for their spiritual progress. Yet he was uniquely able to assist them in their inner development.

The Inspired Wisdom of Gajanana Maharaj
A Practical Commentary on Leading an Effectual Spiritual Life

Presents the teachings and sayings of the great twentieth-century Soham yogi Gajanana Maharaj, with a commentary by Swami Nirmalananda.

The author writes: "In reading about Gajanana Maharaj I encountered a holy personality that eclipsed all others for me. In his words I found a unique wisdom that altered my perspective on what yoga, yogis, and gurus should be.

"But I realized that through no fault of their own, many Western readers need a clarification and expansion of Maharaj's meaning to get the right understanding of his words. This commentary is meant to help my friends who, like me have found his words 'a light in the darkness.'"

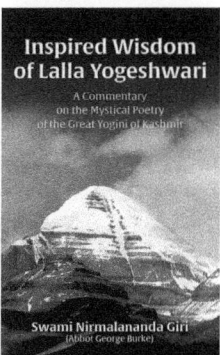

Inspired Wisdom of Lalla Yogeshwari
A Commentary on the Mystical Poetry
of the Great Yogini of Kashmir

Lalla Yogeshwari was a great fourteenth-century yogini and wandering ascetic of Kashmir, whose mystic poetry were the earliest compositions in the Kashmiri language. She was in the tradition of the Nath Yogi Sampradaya whose meditation practice is that of Soham Sadhana: the joining of the mental repetition of Soham Mantra with the natural breath.

Swami Nirmalananda's commentary mines the treasures of Lalleshwari's mystic poems and presents his reflections in an easily intelligible fashion for those wishing to put these priceless teachings on the path of yogic self-transformation into practice.

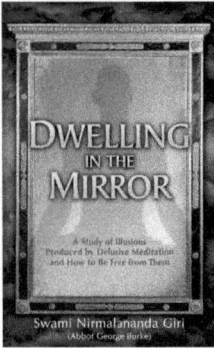

Dwelling in the Mirror
A Study of Illusions Produced By Delusive Meditation
And How to Be Free from Them

Swami Nirmalananda says of this book:

"Over and over people have mistaken trivial and pathological conditions for enlightenment, written books, given seminars and gained a devoted following.

"Most of these unfortunate people were completely unreachable with reason. Yet there are those who can have an experience and realize that it really cannot be real, but a vagary of their mind. Some may not understand that on their own, but can be shown by others the truth about it. For them and those that may one day be in danger of meditation-produced delusions I have written this brief study."

BOOKS ON YOGA & SPIRITUAL LIFE

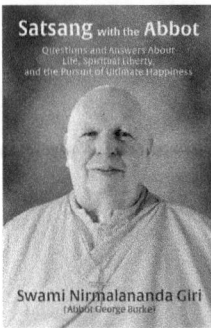

Satsang with the Abbot
Questions and Answers about Life, Spiritual Liberty,
and the Pursuit of Ultimate Happiness

The questions in this book range from the most sublime to the most practical. "How can I attain samadhi?" "I am married with children. How can I lead a spiritual life?" "What is Self-realization?" "How important is belief in karma and reincarnation?"

In Swami Nirmalananda's replies to these questions the reader will discover common sense, helpful information, and a guiding light for their journey through and beyond the forest of cliches, contradictions, and confusion of yoga, Hinduism, Christianity, and metaphysical thought.

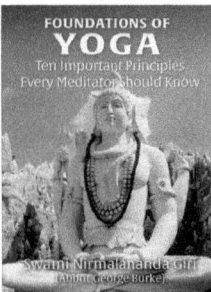

Foundations of Yoga
Ten Important Principles Every Meditator Should Know

An introduction to the important foundation principles of Patanjali's Yoga: Yama and Niyama

Yama and Niyama are often called the Ten Commandments of Yoga, but they have nothing to do with the ideas of sin and virtue or good and evil as dictated by some cosmic potentate. Rather they are determined by a thoroughly practical, pragmatic basis: that which strengthens and facilitates our yoga practice should be observed and that which weakens or hinders it should be avoided.

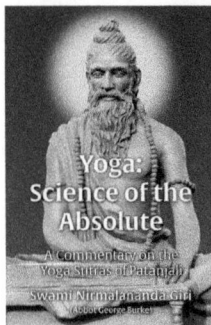

Yoga: Science of the Absolute
A Commentary on the Yoga Sutras of Patanjali

The Yoga Sutras of Patanjali is the most authoritative text on Yoga as a practice. It is also known as the Yoga Darshana because it is the fundamental text of Yoga as a philosophy.

In this commentary, Swami Nirmalananda draws on the age-long tradition regarding this essential text, including the commentaries of Vyasa and Shankara, the most highly regarded writers on Indian philosophy and practice, as well as I. K. Taimni and other authoritative commentators, and adds his own ideas based on half a century of study and practice. Serious students of yoga will find this an essential addition to their spiritual studies.

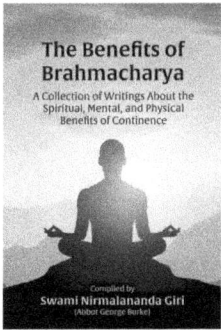

The Benefits of Brahmacharya
A Collection of Writings About the Spiritual, Mental, and Physical Benefits of Continence

"Brahmacharya is the basis for morality. It is the basis for eternal life. It is a spring flower that exhales immortality from its petals." Swami Sivananda

This collection of articles from a variety of authorities including Mahatma Gandhi, Sri Ramakrishna, Swami Vivekananda, Swamis Sivananda and Chidananda of the Divine Life Society, Swami Nirmalananda, and medical experts, presents many facets of brahmacharya and will prove of immense value to all who wish to grow spiritually.

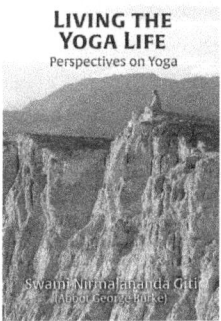

Living the Yoga Life
Perspectives on Yoga

"Dive deep; otherwise you cannot get the gems at the bottom of the ocean. You cannot pick up the gems if you only float on the surface." Sri Ramakrishna

In *Living the Yoga Life* Swami Nirmalananda shares the gems he has found from a lifetime of "diving deep." This collection of reflections and short essays addresses the key concepts of yoga philosophy that are so easy to take for granted. Never content with the accepted cliches about yoga sadhana, the yoga life, the place of a guru, the nature of Brahman and our unity with It, Swami Nirmalananda's insights on these and other facets of the yoga life will inspire, provoke, enlighten, and even entertain.

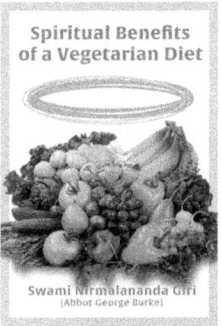

Spiritual Benefits of a Vegetarian Diet

The health benefits of a vegetarian diet are well known, as are the ethical aspects. But the spiritual advantages should be studied by anyone involved in meditation, yoga, or any type of spiritual practice.

Diet is a crucial aspect of emotional, intellectual, and spiritual development as well. For diet and consciousness are interrelated, and purity of diet is an effective aid to purity and clarity of consciousness.

The major thing to keep in mind when considering the subject of vegetarianism is its relevancy in relation to our explorations of consciousness. We need only ask: Does it facilitate my spiritual growth—the development and expansion of my consciousness? The answer is Yes.

BOOKS ON THE SACRED SCRIPTURES OF INDIA

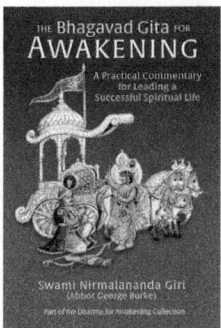

The Bhagavad Gita for Awakening
A Practical Commentary for Leading a Successful Spiritual Life

Drawing from the teachings of Sri Ramakrishna, Jesus, Paramhansa Yogananda, Ramana Maharshi, Swami Vivekananda, Swami Sivananda of Rishikesh, Papa Ramdas, and other spiritual masters and teachers, as well as his own experiences, Swami Nirmalananda illustrates the teachings of the Gita with stories which make the teachings of Krishna in the Gita vibrant and living.

From *Publisher's Weekly*: "[The author] enthusiastically explores the story as a means for knowing oneself, the cosmos, and one's calling within it. His plainspoken insights often distill complex lessons with simplicity and sagacity. Those with a deep interest in the Gita will find much wisdom here."

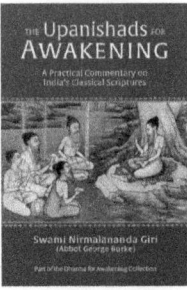

The Upanishads for Awakening
A Practical Commentary on India's Classical Scriptures

The sacred scriptures of India are vast. Yet they are only different ways of seeing the same thing, the One Thing which makes them both valid and ultimately harmonious. That unifying subject is Brahman: God the Absolute, beyond and besides whom there is no "other" whatsoever. The thirteen major Upanishads are the fountainhead of all expositions of Brahman.

Swamiji illumines the Upanishads' value for spiritual seekers from the unique perspective of a lifetime of study and practice of both Eastern and Western spirituality.

The Bhagavad Gita–The Song of God

Often called the "Bible" of Hinduism, the Bhagavad Gita is found in households throughout India and has been translated into every major language of the world. Literally billions of copies have been handwritten or printed.

The clarity of this translation by Swami Nirmalananda makes for easy reading, while the rich content makes this the ideal "study" Gita. As the original Sanskrit language is so rich, often there are several accurate translations for the same word, which are noted in the text, giving the spiritual student the needed understanding of the fullness of the Gita.

All Is One
A Commentary On Sri Vaiyai R. Subramanian's Ellam Ondre

Swami Nirmalananda's insightful commentary brings even further light to Ellam Ondre's refreshing perspective on what Unity signifies, and the path to its realization.

Written in the colorful and well-informed style typical of his other commentaries, it is a timely and important contribution to Advaitic literature that explains Unity as the fruit of yoga sadhana, rather than mere wishful thinking or some vague intellectual gymnastic, as is so commonly taught by the modern "Advaita gurus."

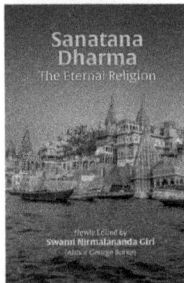

Sanatana Dharma
The Eternal Religion

Sanatana Dharma, commonly called Hinduism, is not just beautiful temples, colorful festivals, gurus and unusual beliefs. It is, simply put, "The Way Things Are" on a cosmic scale. It is the facts of existence and transcendence.

Swami Nirmalananda has edited for the modern reader a book originally printed nearly one hundred years ago in Varanasi, India, for use as a textbook by students of Benares Hindu University. Its original title was *Sanatana Dharma, An Advanced Text Book of Hindu Religion and Ethics.*

A Brief Sanskrit Glossary
A Spiritual Student's Guide to Essential Sanskrit Terms

This Sanskrit glossary contains full translations and explanations of hundreds of the most commonly used spiritual Sanskrit terms, and will help students of the Bhagavad Gita, the Upanishads, the Yoga Sutras of Patanjali, and other Indian scriptures and philosophical works to expand their vocabularies to include the Sanskrit terms contained in these, and gain a fuller understanding in their studies.

The Christ of India
The Story of Original Christianity

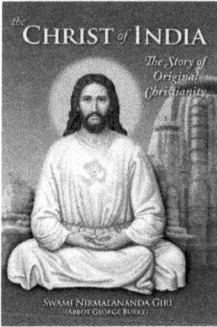

"Original Christianity" is the teaching of both Jesus and his Apostle Saint Thomas in India. Although it was new to the Mediterranean world, it was really the classical, traditional teachings of the rishis of India that even today comprise the Eternal Dharma, that goes far beyond religion into realization.

In *The Christ of India* Swami Nirmalananda presents what those ancient teachings are, as well as the growing evidence that Jesus spent much of his "Lost Years" in India and Tibet. This is also the story of how the original teachings of Jesus and Saint Thomas thrived in India for centuries before the coming of the European colonialists.

May a Christian Believe in Reincarnation?

Discover the real and surprising history of reincarnation and Christianity.

A growing number of people are open to the subject of past lives, and the belief in rebirth–reincarnation, metempsychosis, or transmigration–is commonplace. It often thought that belief in reincarnation and Christianity are incompatible. But is this really true? May a Christian believe in reincarnation? The answer may surprise you.

"Those needing evidence that a belief in reincarnation is in accordance with teachings of the Christ need look no further: Plainly laid out and explained in an intelligent manner from one who has spent his life on a Christ-like path of renunciation and prayer/meditation."—Christopher T. Cook

The Unknown Lives of Jesus and Mary
Compiled from Ancient Records and Mystical Revelations

"There are also many other things which Jesus did, the which, if they should be written every one, I suppose that even the world itself could not contain the books that should be written." (Gospel of Saint John, final verse)

You can discover much of those "many other things" in this unique compilation of ancient records and mystical revelations, which includes historical records of the lives of Jesus Christ and his Mother Mary that have been accepted and used by the Church since apostolic times. This treasury of little-known stories of Jesus' life will broaden the reader's understanding of what Christianity really was in its original form.

Robe of Light
An Esoteric Christian Cosmology

In *Robe of Light* Swami Nirmalananda explores the whys and wherefores of the mystery of creation. From the emanation of the worlds from the very Being of God, to the evolution of the souls to their ultimate destiny as perfected Sons of God, the ideal progression of creation is described. Since the rebellion of Lucifer and the fall of Adam and Eve from Paradise flawed the normal plan of evolution, a restoration was necessary. How this came about is the prime subject of this insightful study.

Moreover, what this means to aspirants for spiritual perfection is expounded, with a compelling knowledge of the scriptures and of the mystical traditions of East and West.

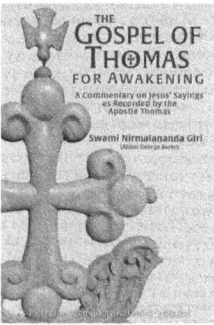

The Gospel of Thomas for Awakening
A Commentary on Jesus' Sayings as Recorded by the Apostle Thomas

When the Apostles dispersed to the various area of the world, Thomas travelled to India, where evidence shows Jesus spent his Lost Years, and which had been the source of the wisdom which he had brought to the "West."

The Christ that Saint Thomas quotes in this ancient text is quite different than the Christ presented by popular Christianity. Through his unique experience and study with both Christianity and Indian religion, Swami Nirmalananda clarifies the sometimes enigmatic sayings of Jesus in an informative and inspiring way.

The Odes of Solomon for Awakening
A Commentary on the Mystical Wisdom of the Earliest Christian Hymns and Poems

The Odes of Solomon is the earliest Christian hymn-book, and therefore one of the most important early Christian documents. Since they are mystical and esoteric, they teach and express the classical and universal mystical truths of Christianity, revealing a Christian perspective quite different than that of "Churchianity," and present the path of Christhood that all Christians are called to.

"Fresh and soothing, these 41 poems and hymns are beyond delightful! I deeply appreciate Abbot George Burke's useful and illuminating insight and find myself spiritually re-animated." –John Lawhn

The Aquarian Gospel for Awakening (2 Volumes)
A Practical Commentary on Levi Dowling's Classic Life of Jesus Christ

Written in 1908 by the American mystic Levi Dowling, The Aquarian Gospel of Jesus the Christ answers many questions about Jesus' life that the Bible doesn't address. Dowling presents a universal message found at the heart of all valid religions, a broad vision of love and wisdom that will ring true with Christians who are attracted to Christ but put off by the narrow views of the tradition that has been given his name.

Swami Nirmalananda's commentary is a treasure-house of knowledge and insight that even further expands Dowling's vision of the true Christ and his message.

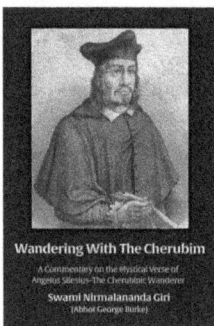

Wandering With The Cherubim
A Commentary on the Mystical Verse of Angelus Silesius–The Cherubinic Wanderer"

Johannes Scheffler, who wrote under the name Angelus Silesius, was a mystic and a poet. In his most famous book, "The Cherubinic Wanderer," he expressed his mystical vision.

Swami Nirmalananda reveals the timelessness of his mystical teachings and The Cherubinic Wanderer's practical value for spiritual seekers. He does this in an easily intelligible fashion for those wishing to put those priceless teachings into practice.

"Set yourself on the journey of this mystical poetry made accessible through this very beautifully commentated text. It is text that submerges one in the philosophical context of the Advaita notion of Non Duality. Swami Nirmalananda's commentary is indispensable in understanding higher philosophical ideas, for Swami's language, while readily approachable, is rich in deep essence of the teachings." –Savitri

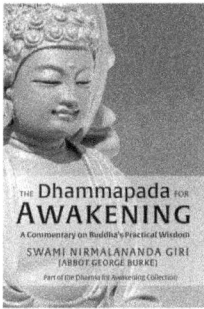

The Dhammapada for Awakening
A Commentary on Buddha's Practical Wisdom

Swami Nirmalananda's commentary on this classic Buddhist scripture explores the Buddha's answers to the urgent questions, such as "How can I find find lasting peace, happiness and fulfillment that seems so elusive?" and "What can I do to avoid many of the miseries big and small that afflict all of us?" Drawing on his personal experience, the author sheds new light on the Buddha's eternal wisdom.

"Swami Nirmalananda's commentary is well crafted and stacked with anecdotes, humor, literary references and beautiful quotes from the Buddha. I have come to consider it a guide to daily living." –Rev. Gerry Nangle

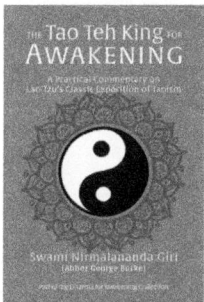

The Tao Teh King for Awakening
A Practical Commentary on Lao Tzu's Classic Exposition of Taoism

"The Tao does all things, yet our interior disposition determines our success or failure in coming to knowledge of the unknowable Tao."

Lao Tzu's classic writing, the *Tao Teh King*, has fascinated scholars and seekers for centuries. Swami Nirmalananda offers a commentary that makes the treasures of Lao Tzu's teachings accessible and applicable for the sincere seeker.

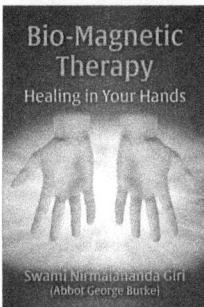

Bio-Magnetic Therapy
Healing in Your Hands

In *Bio-Magnetic Therapy* Swami Nirmalananda teaches the techniques to strengthen your vitality and improve the body's natural healing ability in yourself and in others with specific methods that anyone can use.

Bio-Magnetic Therapy is a simple and natural way to increase the flow of life-force into the body for general good health and to stimulate the supply and flow of life-force to a troubled area that has become vitality-starved through some obstruction. It does not cure; it simply aids the body to cure itself by supplying it with curative force.

How to Read the Tarot
A Practical Method Using the Rider-Waite Deck

Discover Swami Nirmalananda's unique method of reading the Tarot specifically for use with the Rider-Waite deck, with detailed instructions on how to use the cards to develop your intuition for understanding the meanings of the cards. Illustrated with color plates of each of the cards of the Rider-Waite deck with full explanations of their symbolism.

More Titles
The Four Gospels for Awakening
Light from Eternal Lamps
Vivekachudamani: The Crest Jewel of Discrimination for Awakening

9781955046282